The Observer's Pocket Series

BIG BANDS

Observer's Books

The Observer's Book of

BIG BANDS

MARK WHITE

DESCRIBING AMERICAN, BRITISH AND EUROPEAN
BIG BANDS, THEIR MUSIC AND THEIR MUSICIANS
WITH 87 BLACK AND WHITE PHOTOGRAPHS

FREDERICK WARNE

LONDON

First published 1978 by
Frederick Warne (Publishers) Ltd, London
Copyright © 1978 Frederick Warne & Co Ltd

Endpapers: dancing at the Savoy Ballroom, Harlem
(front) and at the Monseigneur Restaurant, London
with Roy Fox (back)

Library of Congress Catalog Card No. 78–62869

ISBN 0 7232 1589 8

Printed and bound in Great Britain by
Morrison & Gibb Ltd, London and Edinburgh

0010·678

CONTENTS

ACKNOWLEDGEMENTS

The author and publishers wish to thank the following for their kind permission to reproduce photographs:

Jazz Journal, pages 29, 32, 59, 67, 70 (right), 156; Gene Lester, page 66; the National Film Archive Stills Library, page 133; Crescendo Publications Ltd, page 111; EMI Music Publishing Ltd, page 14; EMI Ltd, pages 19, 87; Radio Times Hulton Picture Library, pages 44, 47, 48, 54, 94, 96, 98 (both), 100, 106, 107, 154, 166, 169; Raymond Mander and Joe Mitchenson Theatre Collection, page 58; the Bettmann Archive, Inc., New York, N.Y., pages 12, 17, 27, 70 (left), 134, 147, 158, 173; Record Research Magazine Archives, New York, N.Y., page 15; BBC Copyright Photographs, pages 105 (left), 150; Savoy Hotel Press Office, London, page 43; Polydor Ltd, page 113; Decca Record Co. Ltd, page 108.

We are also grateful to *Melody Maker* and Max Jones for the use of their photographic collections.

Picture research: Sandra Assersohn.

FOREWORD

As Mark White is wont to say, he and I have known each other, almost man and boy, these many years. As the guiding light of BBC's *Jazz Club* in earlier days, a record producer, but perhaps more importantly as a man who has an abiding interest in Big Bands, and a collector, he is well-versed to write this book. I only wish he'd decided to do it a long time ago when I was starting out in radio—it would have been of immense help.

An easily-readable guide to a period of popular music that quite relentlessly, and often shatteringly, brought about vast changes in social behaviour. Those effects still ripple through the pond of our entertainment world in the late 1970s.

In the early 1920s dance music was a staple ingredient of the new-fangled wireless. First the cat's whisker and earphones, then those wondrous loud-speakered radios shared out the hitherto exclusive glamour of the smart hotels and ballrooms, carrying it into the humblest homes. For the first time, social and monied barriers were dented as the listener, in imagination, shared the pleasures of the more fortunate at the Savoy Hotel in London, or the Roseland Ballroom in New York.

With the 1930s the Big Bands were in such abundance that their names and styles were as colourful and varied as the hundreds and thousands on a cake frosting—and some were just as ephemeral. Others brought new and imaginative qualities to music in its widest sense.

In the war years, particularly in America, Big

Band activity was at its height. With taxing 'one night stand' tours, and morale-boosting visits to hundreds of service camps, the bands were criss-crossing the nation in such confusion, it's a wonder they didn't all bump into each other. What they did do was bring 'live' music to millions. In tandem, an army of journalists arose to comment and criti-cize, compare and compliment. Views and counter-views were expressed in weighty volumes, and for a researcher as I was, to find a related sequence of facts was often a long and tiresome business.

That's why I would have welcomed a book like this in which Mark White has capsuled the Big Band story and its stars admirably, interlinking the developments and differences in, and between, America and Britain. And it's more than a reference reminder for the already knowledgeable. To a new generation this is an 'open sesame' to that world.

To the purist, the dedicated record collector of long standing, original performances are the only thing, but to today's generation, as well as a large audience of the nostalgic, those immaculate and accurate recreations performed by the Syd Law-rence Orchestra, and the concerts by The Million Airs, have brought more than a small breath of the past to our major concert halls, and allowed us all to discover or relive very special moments of musical history. For the young this is the only way to see and hear a Big Band 'live', in full cry, generating the kind of atmosphere that was all-pervading in, for me, a much missed past.

I know from many letters I receive for my Monday night BBC programmes that there is an increasing number of young people who would like to investigate the Big Band era—this book, I'm sure, will set them on the right road, and prompt further findings.   *Alan Dell, May 1978*

INTRODUCTION

A quick glance at the Bibliography at the back of this book will show you what a great many excellent and authoritative works have been written over the years about the era of the Big Bands. Some cover only the American scene, some only the British and European, one or two touch on both. So far, however, nobody has had the temerity to try to get it all into an 'Observer' book of about 190 pages—including illustrations! Inevitably, therefore, I have to make a few apologies and a few explanations.

First of all, I had to take a quite arbitrary decision about this book along with *The Observer's Book of Jazz*, on which I was working simultaneously. The decision was that, purely for reasons of space, the Jazz book had to be confined to small bands and groups, merely touching on such artists as Ellington and Basie, or Bob Crosby, in spite of knowing full well that they should be in there because they played Big Band Jazz. I have tried to redress the balance by devoting to them as much space as I was able in this book. I hope therefore that the 'Swing purists' will not think that the representation of those bands has been overdone.

Secondly, I would have liked to include much more information about many of the bandleaders listed in the A–Z, particularly their pre-bandleading careers as Jazz musicians. Again, limitations of space prevented this. But you will find much more detail about such musicians as Benny Goodman, Tommy and Jimmy Dorsey, Gene Krupa, Fred Elizalde and others in *The Observer's Book of Jazz*.

Finally, I would like to emphasize that this book has been angled towards the newcomer (and there are many) to Big Band music. When Hubert Gregg had his regular programme *A Square Deal* on BBC Radio 2 some years ago, he received an enchanting letter from a teenager. Hubert had played a Tommy Dorsey record, and the lad wrote to ask: 'Please can you tell me something about this chap Dorsey, and did he ever make any other records? I like his style very much.' I have tried to cater for such as him without, I hope, being so elementary that the aficionados will find little to interest them. In this connection, the Discography is another section that has had to be restricted for lack of space, but at least it is as up-to-date as we could get it at the time of going to press.

Mark White, May 1978

HISTORY

'Do you remember what it was like? Maybe you were there in New York two thirds of the way through the thirties, when there were so many great bands playing. You could go to the Manhattan Room of the Hotel Pennsylvania where Benny Goodman, the man who started it all, was playing with his great band, complete with Gene Krupa. You could go to the Terrace Room of the Hotel New Yorker, and there you'd find Jimmy Dorsey and his Orchestra, with Bob Eberly and Helen O'Connell . . . or to the Blue Room of the Hotel Lincoln to catch Artie Shaw and his band with Helen Forrest . . . or to the Green Room of the Hotel Edison for Les Brown's brand new band. Maybe you'd rather go to some other hotel, like the Palm Room of the Commodore for Red Norvo and Mildred Bailey . . . or to the Grill Room of the Lexington for Bob Crosby and his Bobcats . . . or to the Moonlit Terrace of the Biltmore for Horace Heidt, or down to the Roosevelt Grill for Guy Lombardo and his Royal Canadians. And then there were the ballrooms—The Roseland with Woody Herman and The Savoy with Chick Webb. Not to mention the nightclubs—the Cotton Club with Duke Ellington or the Paradise Restaurant, where a band nobody knew too much about was making sounds the entire nation would soon recognize as those of Glenn Miller and his orchestra.'

That quotation is from *The Big Bands*, by George T. Simon, journalist, author and long time Big Band aficionado. But if you had been in London

A family of musicians, the Noss Company of New Brighton, Pa., photographed about 1890. The family performed as a brass band, chorus and orchestra: each of the children played two or three instruments

and not New York in the thirties, you could have had a similar great choice of music: Lew Stone and his band at the Monseigneur Restaurant with Al Bowlly and Nat Gonella; Ambrose and his orchestra at the Embassy Club with Sam Browne and Elsie Carlisle; Jack Jackson and his new band at the Dorchester Hotel; Sidney Lipton and his band next door at the Grosvenor; Roy Fox and his band at the Café Anglais; Carroll Gibbons and the Savoy Hotel Orpheans, naturally at the Savoy, with Anne Lenner; Jack Harris and his orchestra at Ciro's Club; Harry Roy with his band and his Tiger-ragamuffins at the Mayfair. And as for ballrooms, Joe Loss was about to launch himself on the road to fame at the Astoria.

Of course, to hear all this in person, whether in America or England, cost you money and was for the privileged few. Most people gained their knowledge of and liking for the bands through the media of records and radio. But the surfeit of musical riches available during the thirties had not always been on hand.

'Orchestras for Dancing' there had always been. But 'Dance Bands', and later the 'Big Bands', owed almost nothing to the gavotte, the minuet or the mazurka, and perhaps only a little to the waltz. They owed a great deal however to ragtime which was well and truly in existence by 1897; also to the increasing use of syncopation (developed by and from ragtime, with nuances added later by Jazz pianists); and in particular to the first published sheet music for 'Dance Band Instrumentation' (1911) of the popular tunes of the day. Prior to 1912, the accepted dance combination usually consisted of violin (the lead instrument), piano, drums and banjo. But with printed music available, bands grew in size and soon the accepted instrumentation

13

became something like two or more brass, two or more saxophones (doubling other reed instruments), and a rhythm section of piano, banjo, drums and brass bass (string bass was a later refinement). Often the violin was retained, though with the passing of time it ceased to be a separate player and became an additional double for one of the saxophones. Many of the dance steps of the period were also strongly influenced by the syncopation of ragtime, as well as by the march, the two-step and perhaps the polka. One has only to listen to early records of pieces described as 'A Cakewalk', 'The Bunny Hug', or 'The Grizzly Bear' to discover this. And as the tide of popularity increased the music was taken up by military bands, and they too left something of their imprint on the dance bands that were to follow.

Original American cover of sheet music for the famous song

Gramophone record label of a James Europe number

Then there was the powerful influence of the songwriters. Steeped as many of them were in the music of the Minstrel Shows, Music Hall and Vaudeville, and never slow to make a fast buck, they soon latched onto the fact that America was going dance crazy. So when, in 1911, Irving Berlin wrote *Alexander's Ragtime Band*, a song that has nothing to do with ragtime except its title, the floodgates were opened. But perhaps the final and greatest single influence in the growth of bands was the invention of the fox-trot (*c.* 1912), for with modifications, including the introduction of the slow fox-trot in 1924, it is still with us today. And if an extra push were needed, then it was certainly given by the dancing team of Vernon and Irene Castle, who first performed it so successfully in 1914 that it reached London's 400 Club later that same year.

Many pioneer bandleaders claimed to have invented the dance band, and among those who certainly influenced it even if they did not invent it are such well-known names as Ben Selvin, Wilbur Sweatman, Fred Waring, Art Hickman (the composer of *Rose Room*), and Isham Jones, who had the additional merit of being the first to write his own arrangements instead of using printed parts. But out ahead of them all seems to have been James Europe, a black leader from the early 1900s. He put on a concert at Carnegie Hall in 1914, and was subsequently hired by the fantastically successful Castles as their Musical Director. On America's entry into the First World War he was made an Army Lieutenant, and took a band to France in 1918. He had already recorded for the Victor Company as early as 1915–16. As we have said, the dissemination of early dance music was largely through the medium of records (later radio), although the fact that the musicians, unlike their Jazz counterparts, could read music and play from printed parts speeded up the process enormously. And of course the repertoire helped, based as it was on the popular songs, dances and ballads of the day.

And so to the 1920s, which seem at first sight to belong almost exclusively to Paul Whiteman! But we shall see that that was far from being the case. Nevertheless it is with Whiteman one must start, because even if his was not the first of the Big Bands, he certainly attracted to himself sufficient publicity to give that impression. In fact Paul Whiteman, whose father was a music teacher, started his professional career playing violin in the Denver Symphony Orchestra around 1912. In 1915 he moved to San Francisco, and after brief service in the US Navy as a Musical Director, 1920 saw him leading a dance band for the opening of the Ambassador Hotel in Atlantic City. This was a stroke of fortune indeed, for it was there that the Victor

16

The James Europe Orchestra, 1914

Talking Machine Company elected to hold its annual convention that year, a fact that led directly to the Victor million-selling Paul Whiteman record of *Whispering*, generally accepted as the first popular record to achieve the magic figure.

This success convinced Whiteman that he was onto a good thing, and later that year he moved to New York, opening at the Palais Royal on Broadway for what was to be a lengthy engagement. That the seal of social as well as financial success was

17

impressed on the world of dance music in those early days is made clear by Whiteman in his book *Jazz*. He says: 'We could look out and see the Vanderbilts, Drexel Biddles, Goulds and the rest dancing to our music. Lord and Lady Mountbatten, cousins of the Prince of Wales were among the distinguished guests one night.'

In 1923 the band visited London, playing to a society clientèle at the Grafton Galleries, and on their return home to New York the acclaim that greeted them was such that Whiteman decided the time had come for still greater things. He had already dreamed of a marriage between Jazz and Symphonic music, so he now switched the band's policy to encompass this, culminating in his commission to the then scarcely known George Gershwin to write *The Rhapsody in Blue*. This received its first performance at an historic concert on 12th February 1924 by the Whiteman Orchestra at New York's Aeolian Hall, specially hired by Paul for the occasion, with of course, the composer at the piano. In 1926 the whole circus repeated the performance to a sell-out house at London's Royal Albert Hall, and this was followed by equally successful appearances in Paris, Vienna, and at Berlin's Opera House, the first occasion when such music was heard in those distinguished surroundings.

However, late in 1927 Whiteman reversed his musical policy, reverted to dance music proper, and began the process of signing to his orchestra Jazz musicians, mostly from the recently disbanded Jean Goldkette band. From then on the Whiteman payroll over the years included any number of great Jazzmen such as Bix Beiderbecke, Frank Trumbauer, both Jimmy and Tommy Dorsey, Eddie Lang, Bunny Berigan, Jack Teagarden and Joe Venuti, to name but a few, as well as such pioneering

Paul Whiteman and his Orchestra, 1931

Frank
Trumbauer

Mildred
Bailey

Jazz singers as Red McKenzie and Mildred Bailey. And of course there was his development of The Rhythm Boys—Harry Barris, Al Rinker (Mildred Bailey's brother), and the one and only Bing Crosby. The band remained enormously popular and successful for many years, though it is true to say that as it progressed it became more and more of a show band and less and less a strict dance band. The Swing era began to make it sound dated, but still Whiteman carried on, using various measures and men to up-date his music right through the forties until his retirement in the mid fifties. Even after that he was active in television until his death in 1967.

If we have given undue prominence to Paul Whiteman it is because his influence, his success, and above all the publicity he attracted both to himself and to dance music as a whole were outstanding features of the twenties scene. The result of this was that dance bands began to proliferate throughout America, but it would be entirely wrong to think that every good band was based in New York. We have mentioned Art Hickman. He was based in San Francisco. We have also mentioned Isham Jones who, like Hickman, did a lot of touring, but whose base was quite clearly Chicago and the surrounding area. And if only because of its many broadcasts, as well as its interesting records, one would have to nominate, as the most prominent of all the non-New York bands, The Coon-Sanders Nighthawks. This outfit, based in its early years on Kansas City (later to be the home of the inimitable Count Basie), started its career in 1919, and remained remarkably popular throughout America until the death of Carleton Coon in 1932. Soon after his partner, Joe Sanders, disbanded. They may also have been the first band to pioneer the

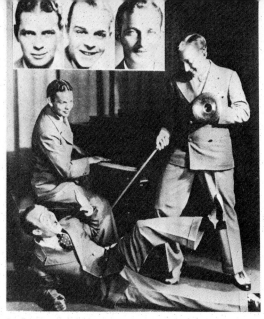

Paul Whiteman's Rhythm Boys: Al Rinker, Harry Barris, Bing Crosby

radio request. The story goes that so popular was their gimmick of inviting listeners to phone in and ask for requests, live on the air, that Western Union installed a ticker tape system between Sanders' piano and Coon's drums to avoid any hold-ups in playing the items!

Earlier we mentioned the name of Jean Goldkette. Born in France in 1899, he lived in America from 1911 until his death in 1962. Perhaps his greatest claim to fame was the astonishing number of Jazz stars he had in his orchestra. Goldkette was fascinated by Jazz and it is commonly considered that it was the enormous cost of his weekly pay-roll of star musicians that led to the downfall of the band, which basically started in Detroit in 1921 and collapsed financially in 1927 after a magnificent farewell performance at the Roseland Ballroom in New York. It is also said that the records it left behind do not do it justice. Well, if nothing other than Bix Beiderbecke's playing on *Clementine* survived it would deserve a place in our annals, to say nothing of the leader's perspicacity in developing the arranging talents of Bill Challis and Don Murray, both later to find fame with Paul Whiteman.

Another Jazz orientated band to find some success in the twenties was that led by Chicagoan ex-drummer Ben Pollack. After being featured with many Jazz groups in his home area, Pollack organized his first band for a date in California in

The Jean Goldkette Orchestra, 1926–7. Well-known members include Bill Challis, the arranger (left), Bix Beiderbecke (fourth from left), Frank Trumbauer (extreme right on roof)

Ben Pollack and his Park Central Hotel Orchestra. Well-known members include Jack Teagarden (back row, second from right), Benny Goodman (centre of front row), Gil Rodin (second from right in front row). Ben Pollack is seated

1925, and by 1927 had begun a highly successful engagement at New York's Park Central Hotel. Included in the personnel were such musicians as Benny Goodman, Glenn Miller, Jimmy McPartland and Gil Rodin. Pollack's main problem was that as a Jazz musician he wanted to feature his soloists, but realized that this was not the road to commercial success, and the ensuing disagreements and compromises resulted in the band's downfall. It is interesting though, that with various changes in personnel Pollack kept going until about 1934, and it was the nucleus of that last band which, under Gil Rodin's management, became welded into the fantastically successful Bob Crosby Orchestra of the late thirties whose speciality was—playing big band versions of Jazz classics!

Because this book is about the Big Bands, and that really means those that reached the height of their popularity in the Swing era of the thirties and forties, we have tended to concentrate so far on dance bands of the twenties whose musical policies were influenced by Jazz. We must not omit to mention however the tremendous popularity of the so-called Sweet bands which started in the twenties, for it is an interesting facet of this scene that throughout the history of popular music there have been two streams running parallel. While fans were rushing to see, hear, buy records of and dance to the great Jazz outfits, there were at the same time millions who enjoyed the small, conventional dance combination of 5–10 pieces.

So, parallel again in the twenties with bands like those of Pollack and Goldkette, there was a whole catalogue of successful orchestras led by such legendary names as Gus Arnheim, Ben Bernie, Abe Lyman, Ben Selvin, Fred Waring, Ted 'is everybody happy' Lewis and numerous others, all purveying 'Sweet Music'. The general style was perhaps best crystallized by Guy Lombardo in the thirties under his famous slogan 'The Sweetest Music this side of Heaven'.

It is usual for Big Band addicts to 'put down' the music of the Sweet bands. Perhaps it is salutary therefore not to forget what Louis Armstrong once said: 'When we were at the Savoy in Chicago in 1928, every Sunday night we'd catch "The Owl Club" with Guy Lombardo, and as long as he played we'd sit right there, Zutty Singleton, Carroll Dickerson and all the band. We didn't go nowhere until Lombardo signed off. That went on for months. Music for me, music that's good, you just want to hear it again.' And as our story progresses it will be seen that these two side-by-side

Guy Lombardo

courses of the Sweet and the Swing have been
evident even into the era of Rock'n'Roll and
modern Pop music.

A further aspect of the Big Band scene that must
not be overlooked was the development of the large
black bands, and the important contribution their
arrangers and musicians made to the music. One
of the earliest and most distinguished arrivals on
the scene was Fletcher Henderson. Born in Georgia,
he arrived in New York in 1920, and by 1924 had
formed a band that took up a residency at the
Roseland Ballroom that was to last for 10 years.
While Henderson was himself a talented pianist,
arranger and composer, his band nurtured such
individual talents as Don Redman, Coleman
Hawkins, Buster Bailey, Jimmy Harrison, Tommy
Ladnier, Benny Morton and, passing through, such
greats as Louis Armstrong, Benny Carter, Rex
Stewart, Roy Eldridge and many more. Records
still exist to testify to the fine performances this band
could and did turn out over the years, and certainly
you did not stay on and on at the Roseland unless
the customers kept coming in droves to dance to
your music.

26

The Fletcher Henderson Orchestra, 1927. Coleman Hawkins seated, centre

But the fact was that in spite of what Paul Whiteman said about the social acceptance of dance music, this did not go in the twenties if your band was black. And the final irony of the Fletcher Henderson story is that having given up his band in the late thirties after various vicissitides, it was his arrangements, specially adapted for the Benny Goodman band and starting with *King Porter Stomp* in 1935, that really sparked off the whole Swing phenomenon. After *King Porter* a string of other fine scores followed, all of which resulted in his joining Goodman as a full time arranger. This achieved for Benny a success that Fletcher was never able to achieve for himself and his own band. Perhaps the Henderson band's finest years were those between 1924 and 1927, for this was the period of Don Redman's association with them, both as saxophonist and staff arranger.

And between 1927 and 1931 Redman was also closely associated with another black band that had a career similar to that of Henderson's—McKinney's Cotton Pickers. Centred on Detroit, in the mid twenties they achieved their greatest fame under Don Redman. Disagreement over policy occurred in 1931 however, resulting in part of the band leaving Redman to form an orchestra, while the remainder stayed on under the direction of yet another ex-Henderson star, Benny Carter. But by 1934 the band was well past its greatest days. Similarly the band of Bennie Moten from Kansas City, which was formed in the early twenties, toured and recorded extensively until the death of its leader in 1935, when the nucleus was taken over by its former pianist William 'Count' Basie, after which their success and development became worldwide.

But the most remarkable career of all the black

bandleaders must be that of the late Edward
Kennedy 'Duke' Ellington. He was born in Washington, D.C. and his early school and college career
in no way suggested the musical prowess that was to
come. In fact, his first working efforts were in the
area of poster design and sign painting, and it was
while working in this way that his natural but
untutored ability to play piano was encouraged. He
began to study harmony, wrote a couple of instantly
forgotten tunes, and began playing as a part time
pianist with a variety of local bands, eventually
teaming up with another local musician, Elmer
Snowden, to form a group called The Washingtonians. In 1923 they secured an engagement at the
Hollywood Club, New York, with Snowden leading
and Duke playing piano.

By the following year however it was Duke who
was leading, with Snowden back in the band

Duke Ellington

playing banjo. Between 1925 and 1927 The Washingtonians played a lot of touring dates, usually in and around the New York and New England areas until their big break came in 1927 with the offer to become resident at the Cotton Club in Harlem, where they stayed until 1931.

The Washingtonians started to make records as early as 1925, and continued to do so in a small way through to the period of their engagement at the Cotton Club, after which their output became almost as legendary as that of Louis Armstrong. Indeed it should be noted that it was prior to 1927 that the first records of several now classic Ellington compositions appeared including *East St. Louis Toodle-oo*, *Birmingham Breakdown*, and especially *Creole Love Call* and *Black and Tan Fantasy*.

George T. Simon in his book *The Big Bands* says: 'When the country started latching on to the big band sounds in the mid 30s, it was merely discovering the music that Duke Ellington and his band had been playing for close on 10 years. Such idolatry heaped upon those "Benny and Artie and Tommy-come-latelys" must have been discouraging for Ellington whose orchestra was, even then, regarded by most musicians and Jazz followers as the best of all the big bands.' As we have seen with other black bands colour had a lot to do with this. The Cotton Club was probably, in its heyday, the most famous entertainment centre in the world. But if its stars were black, most of its audience, especially on opening nights, was white.

Songwriter Harold Arlen, who was commissioned to write the songs for many of the Cotton Club Revues, and who, in the process, gave us such hits as *I've Got a Right to Sing the Blues*, *I've Got the World on a String* and *As Long as I Live* has said: 'The stars of those shows were first and foremost Ethel Waters,

Left: Ethel Waters was one of the early singers at the Cotton Club

Right: Lena Horne began her career there later

Duke Ellington's band, 1936. Left to right: back row, Tricky Sam Nanton, Juan Tizol, Lawrence Brown, Artie Whetsol, Fred Guy; middle row, Barney Bigard, Marshall Royal, Johnny Hodges, Harry Carney, Wellman Braud; front row, Sonny Greer, Duke, Freddy Jenkins (Cootie Williams missing)

and then there was Bill Robinson, and Cab Callo-
way, and Lena Horne—she was about $16\frac{1}{2}$ by the
way, and introduced *As Long as I Live*—and Duke
Ellington had his band there. Those opening nights
were like no other opening nights in the theatre,
because even though it was a night club you'd get
everyone there from Mayor to anybody who was
who. It was like a Broadway opening is today.' (He
said that in the mid sixties.)

After leaving the Cotton Club, the Ellington band
undertook extensive tours of America, and made its
first British and French tour in 1933, then returning
to the US for a further brief stay at the Cotton Club.
But throughout this period almost all the dates were
in theatres and the band was hardly ever booked to
play in hotels or ballrooms for dancing. In fact if you
leave the Jazz fans aside, you could not say that
Duke's band was fully accepted by white audiences
as were the big white Swing bands until his 1943
concert at Carnegie Hall. It is interesting to note
that he had been received by the King and Queen
of England, as well as other European Royalty, long
before his first invitation to visit the White House.

Asked on one occasion how he felt about the fact
that in the thirties his and other black bands were
not considered socially acceptable in hotels, restaurants or ballrooms, Duke said: 'I took the energy
it takes to pout and wrote some blues.' George
Simon describes him as 'a wonderfully warm, witty
and urbane gentleman', and so he was.

In addition it must be said that over the years
Duke always gave credit to his musicians for the
success of his band (his personnel remained more
stable and suffered fewer changes than any other
band in history). Yet those same musicians have
always said that what made the band great was that
Duke was unrivalled not only as a composer/

arranger, but as a leader of men. The lack of the latter quality has caused the downfall of more than one fine band.

We shall be returning to Ellington later in our story, but right now two things must be said. Of all the Big Bands, this was the one that depended almost entirely for its library on the compositions and arrangements of its leader (later those of Billy Strayhorn assumed an ever increasing importance too). Secondly the band never operated quite like any of the others, where a new arrangement would be put in front of the musicians at rehearsal, worked over by the arranger and the leader, maybe altered slightly, and then marked down as the definitive performance. Ellington (and Strayhorn) always wrote with their star musicians at the forefront of their minds. Furthermore, Duke was always willing to accept alterations and suggestions from his musicians long after an arrangement had been finalized. This is one of the reasons why there are so many different versions of the same Ellington composition on record.

But perhaps Duke's greatest influence can be heard not, as one might expect, on other Big Bands (although there are exceptions, e.g. Charlie Barnet), but in the performances of the smaller Jazz groups. It would be invidious to list some and not all of the major contributors to the art of the Jazz solo who learned their trade in the Ellington band. Nevertheless it would equally be unfitting not to recall with respect the names of a few star individuals for their contributions to Jazz and Swing throughout the career of a band that spanned some 40 years. One recalls with sincere affection the work of such men as 'Bubber' Miley on trumpet (the king of the plunger mute); of Joe 'Tricky Sam' Nanton on trombone; Harry Carney on baritone sax; Sonny Greer drums;

Johnny Hodges alto sax; Barney Bigard clarinet; and Jimmy Blanton on bass. In addition there have been, amongst the trumpets: Charles 'Cootie' Williams, Rex Stewart, William 'Cat' Anderson and Ray Nance; in the trombone section Laurence Brown and Juan Tizol; on tenor sax Paul Gonsalves and Ben Webster; on clarinet and alto sax Russell Procope; on drums Louis Bellson; and finally the singers, Adelaide Hall and Ivie Anderson.

We mentioned earlier that the popularity of dance music and later Big Band music was spread mainly by three things: touring and personal appearances by the great bands; their huge successes on gramophone records; and of course radio. In America radio had become commercial in 1922. By the end of 1924 $350 million worth of sets had been sold, and broadcasts, especially what were termed 'remotes' of the bands playing in hotels and ballrooms, would often be networked across the country (allowing for time difference of course). These in turn would boost the sale of the next record, or enlarge the attendance at the next one-night stand.

Most of the name bands, whether their music was of the Sweet or Swing variety, hoped to get some kind of an association going with a local radio station. If these broadcasts proved really popular then their next hope would be to attract a sponsor, who would buy them for a network show (nationwide). Few if any of the black bands were lucky enough to receive this kind of promotion, but without it Big Bands from Fred Waring to Benny Goodman would not have achieved their places in history.

A good example which sums up the situation was the Coon-Sanders Nighthawks. Starting in the very early twenties with a series over station WDAF in Kansas City, by the late twenties they were spending every winter season at the Blackhawk Hotel in

Chicago and broadcasting every night from there over station WGN. This in turn led to a weekly half hour over the whole NBC network.

During the early thirties few changes in the Big Band scene would have been noticeable to an observer who had gone along with the music throughout the late twenties. Historians attach significance to the depression of 1929 and the Wall Street crash, maintaining that this produced a sub-conscious desire for the Sweet music that kept on

Ella Fitzgerald with Chick Webb at the Savoy

coining money for its promoters. But in fact, though bands fell by the wayside they were quickly replaced by others in both spheres of music. Certainly the thirties were the big years for Guy Lombardo and his Royal Canadians. Certainly too, new Sweet music bands quickly became successful: Hal Kemp, Eddie Duchin and Wayne King to name but three. But Whiteman, Waring, Reisman and Lyman kept going too.

And in the area that was shortly to become known as Swing the story was the same. By 1934 Jimmie Lunceford, arguably the best of all the black bands except Ellington, had arrived from Memphis to take up residency at the Cotton Club and to challenge such bands as Fletcher Henderson and McKinney's Cotton Pickers. Even in 1931 Chick Webb, who had arrived in New York in the mid twenties from Baltimore, began his now famous residency at Harlem's Savoy Ballroom—a combination of venue and musicians that not only gave us the Swing standard *Stompin' At The Savoy*, but introduced us to the now much loved voice of the one and only Ella Fitzgerald.

Similarly among the white bands nobody paid much attention to the formation in 1929 by Glen Gray of the Casa Loma Orchestra, a band which, mainly through the scores of its arranger Gene Gifford, was to have the same kind of influence on white Swing as Fletcher Henderson did on black. Indeed, not many people stood up to salute when those two famous brothers Jimmy and Tommy Dorsey combined their talents to form the Dorsey Brothers Orchestra in 1934. Yet, had they not done so, it is unlikely that the Tommy or Jimmy Dorsey Big Bands would ever have existed. Again, these and other new arrivals on the scene did not put such established stalwarts as Isham Jones out of business.

Indeed the man most American musicians were talking about in 1934 had arrived from England to lead a band of all-stars specially picked for him by Glenn Miller. It included Miller himself and Will Bradley on trombones; Charlie Spivak and Pee-Wee Erwin trumpets; Bud Freeman and Johnny Mince among the reeds; and Claude Thornhill (later to lead a fine band of his own) on piano. The leader's name of course was Ray Noble, and he brought with him from England his drummer, Bill Harty, and a singer, described as 'The English Bing Crosby' who soon captured America's hearts—Al Bowlly. The experiment arose from the fact that several of Ray Noble's records of his own compositions (*The Touch of Your Lips, Love is The Sweetest Thing, The Very Thought of You* etc.) had become big hits in the US, although in England Noble's was purely a studio

Ray Noble

band. They opened at the most exclusive spot in New York, The Rainbow Room, 65 floors up the RCA building, and for a couple of years they were very successful. But those who thought that with the galaxy of Jazz soloists in the band they would hear some swinging music were in for a disappointment. Their speciality was ballads, and it was the Sweet bands who needed to worry.

Nevertheless the Swing era was just around the corner, and unwittingly setting the scene for the adulation that was to come for the Goodmans, The Dorseys, the Jameses and the Krupas—a kind of success they were never to know themselves—were the Casa Loma Orchestra. This white band, originally Detroit based, was perhaps the first to achieve some fame without a lengthy residency in any one spot. They did indeed have resident

Al Bowlly

The Casa Loma Orchestra, mid-1940s

bookings across the States for many weeks at a time—summer seasons at the Glen Island Casino and winter bookings at New York's Essex House are two examples. But mostly they were a touring, one-night-stand band, and one which more than any other at that time owed its success to a series of gramophone records.

These were the product, as we have said, of arranger Gene Gifford, and fell into two categories. there were the finely executed ballads such as *Under a Blanket of Blue*, and *It's The Talk of The Town*, and even more importantly there were the 'Swingers', appealing mainly to a young collegiate audience. It was these originals like *Casa Loma Stomp*, *Black Jazz*, *White Jazz*, and *The Maniac's Ball* that were the influential ones.

Indeed so closely did the career of the Casa Loma Orchestra mirror what was to come that they were even the first Swing band to get a radio series. This was the *Camel Caravan* show, which just a few years later was to be such a mainstay of the Benny Goodman band. In fact Benny ran them very close indeed, for prior to his booking on the *Camel Caravan* his band had been signed for a series sponsored by The National Biscuit Company called *Let's Dance*, from which Benny ultimately took his signature tune.

Albert McCarthy in his book *The Dance Band Era* says: 'Whereas many events in the annals of dance music are shrouded in confusion and doubt, it would not be unreasonable to pinpoint the beginning of the Swing era to the evening of 21st August 1935 at the Los Angeles Palomar Ballroom.' Of this there can indeed be little doubt, and as that date marks the beginning of a whole new era this is perhaps the appropriate point at which to look back in time at what had been happening outside America during the years we have covered so far.

As with Jazz, so also in the case of dance music, Britain was the country to follow most closely and in some cases to mirror remarkably accurately what had happened in the US. In *The Observer's Book of Jazz* we were able to trace the emergence of Jazz in Britain directly and quite straightforwardly to the appearance in London in 1919 of the Original Dixieland Jazz Band from America. Unfortunately no such neat procedure can be applied to tracing the rise of dance music—indeed there is a school of thought that believes it owes more than has previously been credited to that same event.

Certain things can however, be stated with reasonable accuracy: for instance, that the Savoy Hotel in London was unquestionably one of the earliest venues for the music. It had certainly catered for dancing since the First World War, and in 1922 created something of a stir by engaging The Savoy Havana Band, led by the American saxophonist Bert Ralton, who had just left Art Hickman's band to look for fame and fortune in Europe.

In the following year the newly formed BBC broadcast its first 'programme of dance music', the honour going to a band led by Marius B. Winter. Within a month the Savoy Havana Band had followed him, and in a further five months became the first band to have a regular series. From which it can be seen that broadcasting began to play an equally important role in the promotion of the music in England as had been the case in America. By the end of 1923 Ralton had left for Australia, and the main band at the Savoy became the now immortal Savoy Orpheans led by Debroy Somers, while the Havana Band stayed on in second place led by Reg Batten.

During the next few years both bands had their share of well known British and imported American musicians. England's Max Goldberg, Tony Thorpe and Billy Mayerl appeared with the Havana Band, as did Rudy Vallee from the US, although at that time he was engaged as an alto sax man, and was not well known as a singer. And among the early members of the Orpheans were Carroll Gibbons, who came over from America in 1923 (he assumed direction of the band in 1927), along with the American trumpeter Frank Guarante, and the three brothers Al, Ray, and Rudy Starita, names which were to become household words in British dance music during the later twenties.

In fact, although no one American band seems to have been responsible for influencing British musicians by its presence here, individual musicians did exert influence, frequently coming over to play and staying for varying periods of time. Some of course, like Carroll Gibbons and Roy Fox, never went home. This is not to say that complete bands never came to England. In 1923 Paul Specht played a season at Lyons Corner House (probably with

Savoy Orpheans conducted by Debroy Somers. Carroll Gibbons at piano

Frank Guarante in the band); Paul Whiteman was also here in 1923, and of course came again to play his now classic Albert Hall concert in 1926. And in 1925 Ted Lewis brought a band over to play at the Kit-Kat Club which contained both Muggsy Spanier and Georg Brunis.

But one of the major developments was the startling invitation extended by the Savoy Hotel in 1927 to Fred Elizalde, the Spanish/American pianist then resident in England, to take what amounted to a band of Jazz musicians into their ballroom to play opposite the Orpheans. This event had great significance for the future of Jazz in Britain. Elizalde had just created something of a furore by forming a Jazz band while still an undergraduate at Cambridge—Fred Elizalde and His Varsity Band, from the Quinquaginta Club, Cambridge—and featuring it in the current Footlights revue. He had made a

Jack Hylton's Orchestra

few records, and was becoming something of a 'darling' among the avant-garde.

Having paid a quick visit to America to sign up musicians, Elizalde opened at the Savoy to an incredulous audience, leading some of the greatest names from both sides of the Atlantic. From the US he had Chelsea Quealey trumpet, Bobby Davis alto sax and Adrian Rollini bass sax; while from the UK came a teenaged Norman Payne on trumpet, Harry Hayes on alto sax and clarinet, Rex Owen tenor sax, Len Fillis guitar, Ronnie Gubertini drums and of course Elizalde himself at the piano.

Later the band was augmented by additional musicians from both countries. The Americans were Max Farley alto sax, Fud Livingston and Arthur Rollini on clarinets and tenors, and Jack Russin piano. The British contingent contained Phil Cardew on alto, George Hurley and Benjamin Frankel violins, and Al Bowlly on guitar. They made a number of broadcasts and some excellent records, but there appear to have been continual disagreements between Elizalde and the musicians on the one hand, and the Savoy management, the BBC, and the record company on the other, over musical policy. The result was that this splendid experiment was regrettably short lived.

Probably the most important British name of this period is that of Jack Hylton. Born near Bolton in 1892, he arrived in London in 1913, and after working as a relief pianist at various clubs and spending the war years in the entertainment division of the Army, he took on his first important job in 1920 as pianist with the Queen's Hall Roof Orchestra. The following year he was already making records under his own name (clearly influenced by early Paul Whiteman recordings), and from then until 1926 he had a band resident at various locations such as the Grafton Galleries, the Piccadilly Hotel and the Kit-Kat Club. During this period Hylton, like Whiteman, began attracting numerous excellent musicians onto his payroll, including trombonist Lew Davis, and later trumpeter Jack Jackson, violinist Hugo Rignold, alto sax and clarinettist E. O. Pogson, and tenor saxophonist Billy Ternent, who later developed into the band's arranger, and subsequently led one of Britain's best known orchestras until his death in 1977.

In many ways Hylton's career was, knowingly or unknowingly, modelled on that of Paul Whiteman. Like Whiteman he attracted good Jazz players to his band; again like Whiteman, about 1926 he gave up his policy of playing straightforward dance music and set out to form what in modern terms we would now call a Showband. They toured the variety theatres of Britain extensively for many years putting on shows which, as entertainment, rivalled if they did not surpass anything to be seen anywhere else in the world—including America. For example, the band toured Europe 16 times between 1927 and 1938, and as early as 1928 Jack is reputed to have turned down an offer of £40,000 for the exclusive services of the band for one year at London's Empire Cinema in Leicester Square.

As to the spectacular nature of their 'production numbers', the story is told of a complete desert set being designed for their interpretation of *Sahara*. The singer of this opus (probably Pat O'Malley) made his entrance riding a real camel, and dressed as a Sheik in the Valentino manner. It is reported to have stopped the show, especially on the occasion in one theatre when the man in charge of the camel neglected to give it the opportunity of relieving itself before going on stage. This it proceeded to do backstage just before its cue, fusing the footlights

Ambrose (vln) and his band at the Mayfair Hotel, London, 1932

and plunging the stage into darkness in the process!

Two attempts to present the band in America failed. In 1929 they should have appeared at New York's Paramount Theatre, but a threatened strike by the theatre's pit musicians put paid to that. And in 1935 the band actually arrived in New York only to be faced with a ban by the American Federation of Musicians which prevented them from appearing. It did not however prevent the musicians visiting many of the city's famous Jazz spots before taking the return boat home, and it did not prevent Hylton himself fulfilling engagements to rapturous applause, with a band of American musicians but including his own speciality acts who had accompanied him from England. These included Billy Ternent as his arranger, Alec Templeton (the blind pianist), and singers Peggy Dell, Eve Becke and Pat O'Malley.

Jack Payne's band in 1927

Running parallel with the rise to fame of Jack Hylton were the fortunes of Bert Ambrose. Born a Londoner in 1897, he went to America while quite young, learned to play the violin and obtained work at the New York Palais Royal, where he was heard by the owner of the Embassy Club in London and persuaded to return home and put in a band there. This he did with considerable success in 1922. Broadcasting was not allowed by the club management, but recording was. Ambrose gradually made changes in his personnel (the addition of Joe Crossman on alto sax and clarinet was greatly to his advantage).

His records began to achieve some success, so when in 1927 he was offered the opportunity to take an enlarged band into the Mayfair Hotel that organization had to pay him the then astonishing figure of £10,000 per year. Again a mixture of the best British and American musicians helped to set the seal on these early successes. Among the local contingent were Joe Crossman of course, Ted Heath and Sydney Lipton, both later to find fame in their individual ways; pianist/arranger Bert Read; Max Bacon, the drummer who later turned comedian; and Jack Miranda and Dennis Radcliffe.

From America came Joe Brannelly on banjo/guitar, Perley Breed on alto sax, clarinettist Danny Polo, and Sylvester Ahola, a trumpeter much in the Nichols/Beiderbecke tradition. The latter appeared prolifically on records under various leaders besides Ambrose, and his playing was frequently mistaken for that of Jack Jackson. And the vocalist, Sam Browne, joined the fold and stayed right through to 1945. Broadcasting from the Mayfair was immediately successful, and by 1929 the Ambrose band had already assumed their 10.30 Saturday night spot for the BBC, which was soon to boost them to number one in the nationwide popularity poll of the 1930s.

One other main band which was to influence the music in Britain was that of Jack Payne. His first broadcasts with his band were from the Hotel Cecil where he was resident, and when in 1928 the BBC decided to replace the London Radio Dance Band it was to Payne they turned, to form what was to be the first of a succession of BBC Dance Orchestras. The band contained a number of outstanding musicians including Jack Jackson and E. O. Pogson from the Hylton band, and the talented violinist Eric Siday. Within two years, Payne's schedule of seven broadcasts per week plus recording sessions and, wherever possible, personal appearances with the band at theatres, put him at the top of the tree in public acclaim. In fact the band was never as good as Hylton's, which broadcast less than almost anybody, and certainly by the time Payne left the BBC in 1932 to undertake concentrated variety appearances, he had long been overtaken in musical terms by Ambrose.

In summing up the close of the decade in America we said that an observer who had stayed with the music scene through the late twenties into the early or middle thirties would not have been aware of much change in the music. This statement would be much less true if applied to Britain. Bands in this country had never slotted as easily into categories as they had in the States. For one thing there was not the Jazz tradition spurring the musicians on. For another there was not the element of black music which so sharply divided both bands and fans in America. Typical running orders for broadcasts, selections of titles for records, or programmes of music for an evening's dancing would contain a real mixture of styles. There would be Jazz-orientated arrangements of such Dixieland tunes as *Eccentric* (the Savoy Orpheans made a typical recording of this one), or *Milenburg Joys* (Jack Hylton's Kit-Kat Club Band made a good example). And these would be side by side with the popular ballads of the day, such as Ambrose's version of *Body and Soul*, and liberal helpings of 'novelty' or comedy items—Jack Payne's much requested *Muckin' About in The Garden*, for instance.

Also, the depression of the thirties did have a noticeable influence here whereas that is not so clearly established in the States. The effect in Britain seemed to be that the public became more attuned to bands with some pretensions to Swing—Hylton, Stone, Fox, Ambrose—rather than to the Sweet bands. And of course, because Britain is so small by comparison with America, the financial

Roy Fox and some of his band

squeeze was felt outside London rather than in the exclusive West End night spots where most of the best bands played.

Certainly during the first five years of the thirties, immediately prior to the advent of Swing in the States, significant changes began to happen on the British dance band scene. It was during this period that Hylton and Payne were competing against each other for the title 'Britain's greatest Showband' at variety theatres up and down the country (I think Hylton always won). Henry Hall had succeeded Payne as the next leader of the BBC Dance Orchestra. His policy was not all that different, but if anything he was closer to the Sweet bands of America.

Roy Fox had arrived from America in 1930 and after an unsuccessful début at the Café de Paris, he was invited to form a band for the opening of the Monseigneur Restaurant in Jermyn Street. This he did with a veritable all-star line-up that included Nat Gonella and Sid Buckman, trumpets; Joe Ferrie, trombone; the two Amstells, Micky and Billy, on altos with Harry Berly on tenor, Lew Stone on piano, Bill Harty on drums and Al Bowlly guitar and vocals.

Within five months however Fox had been taken seriously ill and had to spend a lengthy spell recuperating. During this time the band was taken over by Lew Stone, and although Fox returned when he was better, disagreements with the management arose and he left in 1932 to form a new band for the Café Anglais. He took with him only Sid Buckman, leaving the remainder at the Monseigneur under Lew Stone's direction.

Better luck now took over for Fox, and after a success at the Café Anglais he moved to the Kit-Kat Club, and the combination of an excellent band

together with prolific recording and broadcasting soon had his name at the top of the tree.

Meanwhile the band left at the Monseigneur under Stone also went from strength to strength and by 1933, with a personnel that now included Lew Davis on trombone, Joe Crossman, Jim Easton and Ernest Ritte among the saxes, Eddie Carroll on piano, and Tiny Winters on bass plus many other stalwarts, this band and Ambrose's were generally regarded as the most musicianly in the country. The secret of the success of the Stone band seems to have been its mixed repertoire. It specialized in copies of

The Harry Roy Dance Band. Harry Roy at centre, offering cigarettes

the famous Casa Loma instrumentals (*White Jazz, Blue Jazz* etc.), hardly anyone in England at that time having heard of the Casa Loma Orchestra. It also had trumpet and vocal features for Nat Gonella, and the best of the ballads of the day sung by Al Bowlly. This was all combined with such style that soon their BBC spot at 10.30 on Tuesday nights was rivalled only by Ambrose's on Saturdays.

Ambrose had a band of equal musicianship which still included Danny Polo, Dennis Radcliffe and Max Bacon, and to which he had added the talents of Ted Heath on trombone, Max Goldberg on trumpet, and Sid Phillips who not only played baritone sax, but who was gradually becoming responsible for more and more of the band's best arrangements. Although its sound was quite different from that of the Stone band Ambrose's repertoire was not dissimilar. A mixture of swinging instrumentals (many composed by Sid Phillips as well as arranged by him), features for its soloists, especially Max Bacon's drumming and comedy singing, and excellent vocals from a team that included faithful Sam Browne and vivacious Evelyn Dall. All this was happening before that famous date—21st August 1935—at the Palomar Ballroom Los Angeles.

Once again we take that as our starting point for a new era of music, but before we return to the States to look at what happened in detail, one or two other things must be mentioned. If you care to draw a musical parallel between the two countries, you could compare the performances of Hylton and Payne with those of Whiteman; Ambrose, Fox and Stone perhaps with the bands of Isham Jones, the Dorsey Brothers, and the Casa Loma; while Henry Hall, Carroll Gibbons and the Savoy Orpheans, and Ray Noble could be compared with the major Sweet bands of America. Incidentally, Noble never had a residency in England. It was a band that only existed for recording, broadcasting and concert engagements. Finally, several new bands appeared on the London scene between 1930 and 1935, and we must not leave them out.

Harry Roy who, with his brother Sid, had been around since the mid twenties, got his break into the big time with the opportunity of taking a band into the Café Anglais in 1933, and a successful recording and broadcasting career immediately followed. There has been a tendency among critics to 'put down' the Harry Roy band, mainly I believe for two reasons. The first was Harry's natural flamboyance, corny singing (he was billed as 'The King of Hot-Cha'), and almost equally corny clarinet playing. The second was the distinctive pseudo-ragtime sound of the band, caused partly by its feature of two pianists (the Tiger Ragamuffins), partly by the emphasis on such numbers as *12th Street Rag* in its repertoire.

Nevertheless, not only was it highly popular with the public who listened to its regular broadcasts and bought its records, it also contained some excellent musicians. These included Norman White and Stanley Black as the two pianists who succeeded the original pair Ivor Moreton and Dave Kaye, and latterly drummer Ray Ellington and clarinettist Nat Temple. When given the right material they could collectively come up with performances of a very high standard. Harry Roy later embarked on a successful tour of variety theatres with a show that attempted to rival the 1920s spectaculars of Jack Hylton. At the time of his marriage to Princess Pearl, the daughter of the then white Rajah of Sarawak, he used to make his stage entrance riding on an elephant—with memories of Jack Hylton's camel in mind perhaps?

Another band in the same general category as Harry Roy's was that of Billy Cotton, although the difference between the two men as individual personalities was infinite. Cotton's first steps along the road to fame came in 1928 when his band was booked into the Astoria Ballroom. From there it moved to the Locarno Streatham, and then to Ciro's Club. But by the mid thirties Billy had given up any idea of remaining a dance band for dancing, and had started on the career which was ultimately to make him so enormously successful as a touring stage band specializing in comedy routines laced with straight numbers as well, though without any attempt to copy the magnificence of the Hylton shows.

In addition those same five years saw the emergence of three Sweet styled bands: Maurice Win-

The Billy Cotton band

nick, whose avowed intention was to sound more like Guy Lombardo than Guy Lombardo; Sydney Lipton, who had an extremely well drilled and personable band playing in the ballroom of the Grosvenor House Hotel; and perhaps the most surprising of all, a band formed for the opening of the Dorchester Hotel in 1933 by trumpeter Jack Jackson, a residency which he maintained, one must report, until 1939. The surprise of this band was that in no way could it be called a Swing outfit in the sense that the word might have been applied (although it wasn't) to Ambrose or Lew Stone—surprising because of Jackson's avowed personal dedication to Bix Beiderbecke and Red Nichols. Nevertheless, the sweet, smooth, yet highly rhythmic style he adopted was a delight to the patrons of the

Dorchester as the length of his stay shows, and as the records he left behind testify.

This was the state of affairs in London, then, in the mid thirties. And as a radio announcer of the period might have said: 'We take you now to the Palomar Ballroom, Los Angeles, and the music of Benny Goodman and his Orchestra.'

Benny formed his first band in 1934 after a 10-year career of ever increasing stature as a Jazz clarinettist. A summary of his achievements are listed under A–Z, so let us just say here that the band's first series of touring dates had begun in May 1935. By the time 21st August had arrived, and they found themselves on the stand at the Palomar Ballroom, not only the musicians, but Benny too could be forgiven for thinking that the whole tour was going to be little short of disaster, and that the Palomar booking would be no different from those that had preceded it. In Denver for instance, the ballroom manager

Jack Jackson,
1936

Benny
Goodman,
1945

had insisted they switch to waltzes in an attempt to stem the flood of patrons demanding their money back. Drummer Gene Krupa later recalled of the Palomar date: 'We played the first couple of sets under wraps. We weren't getting too much reaction, so Benny, I guess, decided to hell with playing it safe and we started playing numbers like *King Porter Stomp*.' This was the now famous Fletcher Henderson arrangement.

George T. Simon in *The Big Bands* reports: 'The engagement was a smash. Kids gathered round the bandstand and screamed for more. Swing was really in.' NBC's mics picked up the broadcast and this reaction, with the result that the remainder of the tour was transformed into a howling success and concluded with what should have been a three-week booking at Chicago's Congress Hotel turning into a stay of eight months. To quote George T. Simon again: 'When they finally left, there was only one thing the management could do for a follow up: it closed the room and re-decorated it!'

The highlights of the careers of those who followed swiftly in the footsteps of Benny Goodman are encapsulated in our A–Z. To quote a line from the lyric of Kurt Weill's song *Mack The Knife*, 'The line forms on the right dear': Tommy and Jimmy Dorsey, Glenn Miller, Les Brown, Bob Crosby, Harry James, Gene Krupa, Artie Shaw, Woody Herman, Charlie Barnet—to name just some of the pace-setters. In this section of the book we concern ourselves with styles and trends.

We referred earlier to the two parallel streams of popular music in the band idiom flowing alongside each other—the Jazz-orientated dance bands, and the Sweet bands. From now on it is possible to redefine this as virtually three streams. The Sweet bands continued almost unchanged throughout the thirties, and in many cases on through the forties, hardly modifying their successful styles at all. Thus, apart from the big improvements in recording and playing technique, records by say, Guy Lombardo or Lawrence Welk from the late forties or early fifties, are indistinguishable in style from their performances of 20 years earlier. Then you have the white Swing bands, absorbing the Jazz-orientated influences to which we have just referred and going on from strength to strength. And lastly the big black bands, stemming as we have seen mostly from Fletcher Henderson, and now beginning to attract to themselves something of the aura of the white bands in terms of public acceptance. In particular, we have already noted Duke Ellington and Chick

Webb. Following in quick succession came Jimmie Lunceford, Lionel Hampton, and others, culminating in the incredible success of Count Basie in the late thirties which he has maintained right through into the seventies.

Some critics make no distinction of colour between categories 2 and 3, lumping both black and white bands together under the heading 'Big Band Jazz'. There is some justification for this, but it leaves out the tremendous differences in style and sound between these black bands and their white counterparts.

For these, two main things were responsible. First, the approach to music differed considerably between the black and white musicians, and this was in many ways identical to the difference between the black and white styles in Jazz. Secondly, and of vital importance, was the role of the arranger. We have seen that it was the arrangements supplied to Benny Goodman by Fletcher Henderson that produced the remarkable volte-face of August 1935. Soon Goodman was to begin using other distinctive writers as well: Edgar Sampson (also the composer of such hit instrumentals as *Blue Lou* and *Don't Be That Way*); Jimmy Mundy (whose scores may well have been responsible for the introduction of the descriptive phrase 'killer-diller'!); and later still, Eddie Sauter of Sauter/Finegan Orchestra fame; and Mel Powell. Each contributed something fresh, and at the same time helped to give an instantly recognizable style to the sound of the band.

Of course, the Goodman band was not without its changes in personnel. As musicians came and went, Benny would expect his arrangers to take into account the strengths and weaknesses of his men. Soon still other significant things began to happen. In 1936 for instance, Teddy Wilson joined the band

61

Peggy Lee

on piano replacing Jess Stacy. Not only did this mark the start of the immortal Benny Goodman Trio, later to be followed by the Quartet and the Sextet, it also marked the first occasion when a black musician became accepted by the public as a member of an otherwise wholly white orchestra. In this respect Benny was a pioneer, and within a year Wilson had been joined by Lionel Hampton on vibes.

Other important changes began to follow. Late in 1936 Harry James left Ben Pollack's band to join the brass section, and soon he in turn was joined by Ziggy Elman. Singers too began to assume a significance greater than the hitherto traditional one line: 'with vocal refrain by . . .' Goodman had been fortunate in starting out with the services of an accomplished performer, Helen Ward. But when she left to get married, he had some difficulty in finding a suitable replacement before coming up with Martha Tilton. And we must not forget that the arranger was just as important when writing for a vocal performance as in his more obvious role as the creator of another 'killer-diller'. Helen Ward's early recording of *Goody Goody* exemplifies this. The record by Ella Fitzgerald with the Benny Goodman band (she never appeared live with them) of *Goodnight My Love* is now regarded as a classic—not only for its fine singing of an excellent song, but also for its sensitive and complementary setting.

So, for Benny, success followed success, leading to the now legendary Carnegie Hall concert of 1938. Musicians came and went, some to become band-leaders in their own right—Harry James, Gene Krupa, Lionel Hampton, in particular. Others, equally brilliant in different ways, joined. Cootie Williams (from Duke Ellington) and Charlie Christian, both black; Dave Tough; and others of similar calibre. In the vocal department Helen Forrest followed Martha Tilton, and, in 1941, arguably the greatest singer of them all, Peggy Lee, succeeded Helen. Benny, rightly dubbed 'The King of Swing', last had a full-time band during the years 1947–49. Curiously enough, and with the benefit of hindsight, we now know that the great days of the Big Bands were numbered by then anyway, though many struggled on and one or two new ones even had the temerity to try to join the ranks.

We have already recalled how the Dorsey brothers, Tommy of the trombone and Jimmy of the clarinet and alto sax, formed the Dorsey Brothers Orchestra in 1934. Equally, the ever-widening disagreement between them which led to Tommy storming off to form a band of his own in

Tommy Dorsey and his Orchestra including Sinatra and Buddy Rich in the film *Las Vegas Nights*, 1941

1935 is now history. An astrologer might be able to tell us why 1935 was such an important year for Swing. We can only be glad that it happened and record that, following the Benny Goodman phenomenon the next pioneer, chronologically, was Tommy Dorsey.

It seems that the band publicists of the thirties had to tie labels round everybody's necks, and Tommy's was 'The Sentimental Gentleman of Swing'. Partly this was based on his signature tune, *I'm Getting Sentimental Over You.* Partly it was based on the great ability the band displayed in its interpretations of the ballads of the day. To what extent the 'Gentlemanly' part was based on Tommy's own personality is not clear! Certainly he was tempestuous, and never failed to let his musicians feel his full wrath if they did not live up to his perfectionist ideals. In this respect he was totally different from Benny Goodman, whose now well-known method of disciplining his men was to use what has been described succinctly as 'The BG Ray' (Harry James once said: 'A fish-eye stare').

Probably the Dorsey band could be best summed up by the use of the phrase 'all-rounder'. Although as an instrumentalist Tommy frequently disclaimed any ability as a Jazz soloist, the records prove him wrong. They also prove however, what an absolute master of taste and melodic invention he was when playing a ballad. Frank Sinatra learned a great deal about breathing and phrasing from Dorsey's playing. In this connection it is interesting to recall a recording session by The Metronome All-Stars. This was a group of top musicians who had won places in a popularity poll sponsored by the American music magazine. Tommy and Jack Teagarden both found themselves on the session, and were asked by the producer to play a 12-bar

Paul Weston

blues together. Tommy agreed only on condition that he played the melody (improvised) while Teagarden played the Jazz around it. The result was a classic.

In the making of his Big Band, Tommy did all the right things. He knew the importance of distinctive arrangements, and he had working for him both Paul Weston and Axel Stordahl—two of the best. He knew the importance of personable singers, and he hired Edythe Wright and Jack Leonard. Still the start was tough. Their first records were unremarkable (though *Weary Blues* had some success), as were their first appearances in public. Changes began to take place in personnel. In came Dave Tough on drums, Bud Freeman on tenor sax, Bunny Berigan on trumpet, Johnny Mince on clarinet. Their first real breakthrough was probably their now classic recording of *Marie* in January 1937, backed with another title, that brought them almost equal success, *Song of India*. Just to prove that there are exceptions to every rule, it should be reported that Tommy bought the arrangement of *Marie* for a few dollars from an unknown band he heard playing it at a theatre. And the idea for *Song of India* was worked out collectively at rehearsal by himself and some other members of the band!

Finally came that other break they had been waiting for. They had already interspersed the inevitable round of one-night stands and relief bookings for other bands with some radio work. But they wanted a big show. And at last it arrived, in the shape of a chance to be featured on a new programme for Raleigh and Kool cigarettes on the NBC Network. With that and two hit records behind them, and driven as they undoubtedly were by Tommy's larger than life personality, the band could only go forward and it did.

Bunny Berigan

Jo Stafford

Frank Sinatra

As with Benny Goodman there were numerous changes over the years. Passing through the band at one time or another were such names as Yank Lawson, Buddy de Franco, Charlie Shavers and Buddy Rich. On the singing front Edythe Wright was succeeded by Jo Stafford. Jack Leonard was replaced by Frank Sinatra. Sy Oliver joined the arranging staff. The period of the band's life when at one and the same time it contained both Sinatra and Buddy Rich, two of the biggest egos in the band business, must have been quite something. Probably it was only possible because Tommy's was bigger than both! Towards the end of 1942 Frank Sinatra departed, as did Jo Stafford, who by then was Mrs Paul Weston. Buddy Rich was called up into the Marines, and in spite of good replacements (Gene Krupa came in for a while on drums, and Dick Haymes took over the vocal chair), the band did not seem to be making it. Yet, ironically, two of its most successful records were made just two years later in 1944. Buddy Rich had come back from the Marines, Nelson Riddle had joined on trombone (he was only just beginning his arranging career), and there was a first class singing group, The Sentimentalists. The titles were of course *Opus 1* and *On The Sunny Side of The Street*. Following that period, and almost as if he began to see that the writing was on the wall for Big Bands, Tommy began to interest himself more and more in the business side of music, and less and less in the band as such. He died, sadly at the early age of 51, in 1956.

It seems churlish to devote less space to the Jimmy Dorsey Orchestra than to Tommy's. But the facts of life are that, charming as Jimmy may have been and excellent musician though he undoubtedly was, he never seemed to have that desire to will his way

Left: Bob Eberly *Right:* Helen O'Connell

up to the top that always stood his brother in good stead when it came to a crisis. One must however record that his band was indeed a successful one. It had its share of hit records (*Green Eyes, Amapola* and *Tangerine* are three that spring to mind), featuring the popular singing team of Bob Eberly and Helen O'Connell. It had excellent musicians throughout its life and first class arrangers (Toots Camarata was one of its best), and these were backed up by network appearances on radio programmes.

The band broke up in the late forties as did so many others, but in the early fifties Jimmy and Tommy were briefly reunited in a new Dorsey Brothers Orchestra. Those who saw and heard it said three things. First that they had never seen Jimmy so happy as he obviously was to be back sitting in the saxophone section. Secondly that it was a good band, but doomed because the Big Band era was already over. And thirdly that shrewd Tommy recognized that by now Jimmy was at least as popular as he was, so what better than to have a reunion (Jimmy's hit record of *So Rare* was still well loved and remembered). Jimmy outlived his brother by only 6 months, and died in 1957.

The band that logically was the next to follow Goodman and the Dorseys up the ladder of fame was that of clarinettist Artie Shaw. It started life in 1936. That Artie Shaw had all the prerequisites of a successful bandleader was never in doubt. A first class instrumentalist, good looking, an engaging personality, the ability to pick the right musicians (Buddy Rich was his drummer before joining Tommy Dorsey), the right arrangers (Ray Conniff and Claude Thornhill), and the right singers (Helen Forrest, Georgia Gibbs (Fredda Gibson), Tony Pastor, Mel Torme). But Shaw never could come to terms with the business side of music, and this, combined with his mercurial temperament, meant that the band never realized its potential as had those of Goodman and Tommy Dorsey. Shaw was aware that for success the band needed a style. But he seemed to want it instantly, and when it became apparent that a certain course was not getting anywhere, his method was not to modify, but to scrap everything and start again. Thus his second band was formed in 1937, another in 1940, yet another in 1942; in 1943 he went into the US Navy to lead one of the best of the American Service bands, and started another civilian band on his discharge in 1944; he tried again in 1949, and finally in 1953, after which he gave up!

Since Benny Goodman was 'The King of Swing', Shaw's publicists dubbed him 'The King of The Clarinet'. Indeed it is for his personal playing that he is likely to be best remembered on such records as *Concerto for Clarinet*, although the band's most successful records date from 1937: *Begin The Beguine* (arranged by Jerry Gray, later to be such an important figure in the Glenn Miller band), *Indian*

Love Call, *Back Bay Shuffle*, *Nightmare* (the band's signature tune), and subsequently *My Heart Belongs To Daddy* (the singer was Kitty Kallen), and *What is This Thing Called Love* (Mel Torme and The Meltones). There are many 'quotes' of reported sayings by Artie Shaw. Among the best is one alleged to stem from Charlie Christian's success on introducing the electric guitar in the Goodman band: 'All electric guitarists should be electrocuted!'

Between 1935, when the marriage between the Benny Goodman band and the Palomar Ballroom gave birth to Swing, and the beginning of the demise of Swing 10 years later, no fewer than 10 other big name bands rose to fame. We have already discussed four of them. If only there were space within the confines of this book, how nice it would be to record more about Charlie Barnet than

Artie Shaw and his band in the film *Second Chorus*, 1940

that this Ellington-inspired band, having started out in the mid thirties, had its first hit in 1939 with its record of Ray Noble's *Cherokee*; that it developed the arranging talents of Billy May; the singing styles of Kay Starr and Fran Warren; the playing of Peanuts Holland, Dodo Marmarosa, Trummy Young, Barney Kessel and Clark Terry; and that it will be best remembered for such recordings as *Pompton Turnpike*, *Wings over Manhattan*, *Redskin Rhumba*, and the never to be forgotten *Skyliner*.

Equally one does miserable justice to a band that was in some ways the most relaxed, swinging and musical of them all—Les Brown and His Band of Renown—by simply recalling that it began in 1936, reached its peak in the late forties, put Doris Day on the map, and left two never to be forgotten records: *Sentimental Journey* (with Doris Day) and *I've Got My Love to Keep Me Warm*.

Then there was the brilliant but quite different Bob Crosby Orchestra. Different because its personnel changed so little and because all of them were great Jazz players. Different too because it was a co-operative band (the boys were all shareholders), and it was the only band of the Swing era to specialize in and popularize Big Band Dixieland. Sax man Gil Rodin was its inspiration and its Managing Director, and he formed it when he and a nucleus of other good men found themselves out of work after Ben Pollack disbanded. They hired Bing Crosby's brother Bob as their singer and 'front man', and from their début in 1936 never looked back until, in common with so many bands, the war years gradually saw the stability of their personnel diminished, and the end finally came in 1942.

To two other stalwarts of the Swing era we also have to do far less than justice—Harry James and Gene Krupa. Gene left Benny Goodman to form

Gene Krupa

his own band in 1938. To be, as he then was, probably the finest drummer in the world, as well as being an extremely good looking and personable guy who was idolized by his fans, seemed a good enough reason for doing it. In fact the band had many ups and downs. Apart from Gene's drumnastics, it will probably be best remembered for launching Anita O'Day (one of the very best of the era's Jazz singers), for the trumpet playing of Roy Eldridge, for some outstanding records such as the instrumental *Leave Us Leap*, and the marvellous vocal duet between Buddy Stewart and Dave Lambert called *What's This?* Of the titles Anita O'Day made with the band, *Murder He Says*, and the now classic duet with Eldridge, *Let Me Off Uptown*, will live on.

Harry James, who joined the Benny Goodman band in 1936 and did much to give it its brass style, left in 1939 to form his own band. Throughout its career it has been associated with fine musicians, and it will forever be remembered for the sensational James trumpet style, and for launching first Frank Sinatra (it was from James that he moved to Dorsey), then Helen Forrest, then Dick Haymes. In fact the recipe for most of Harry James' hit records was arrangements that were positively written to promote the unique blend of trumpet plus vocal styling. His record of *You Made Me Love You* remains personally associated with him, but we recall with pleasure such Helen Forrest hits as *I Don't Want to Walk Without You*, *I Had The Craziest Dream* and *I've Heard That Song Before*. The only Sinatra/James title to survive in memory is *All or Nothin' at All*, and frankly, today one wonders at its success, while the two best Haymes titles are probably *A Sinner Kissed an Angel*, and *I'll Get By*. Harry James was a generous boss: he saw Sinatra's star potential, and urged him to go to Dorsey, who could do more for the singer's career.

Anita O'Day

The last few paragraphs have done scant justice to four great bands. But there remain two more white bands of the Swing era to which we must turn our attention, as well as having a look at the scene among the black orchestras. Woody Herman's first band (he didn't call it a 'Herd' then) was born in 1937. It was billed as 'The Band That Plays The Blues', and it did. Not a formula calculated to bring success, as Woody found out from such incidents as one in Houston, Texas, when the ballroom manager sent him a note saying: 'You will kindly stop singing and playing those nigger blues.' Fortunately the band did not, and some of its early records for Decca were quite interesting, though not hits—*Blues Upstairs*, *Blues Downstairs*, and its signature tune *Blue Flame*. Woody's clarinet was a feature of the band, and his style had more than a thought of some of the great black clarinettists in it, so that in no way did his playing conflict with Goodman or Shaw.

Woody
Herman

Real success came in 1939 with a hit record, *Woodchopper's Ball*. Nearly 40 years later it is still Herman's most requested number. With that behind them they began to get some good bookings, taking over from Glenn Miller for a summer season at Glen Island Casino, a venue which had just been the scene of Miller's first major success. When this was followed by bookings at Chicago's Sherman Hotel, and dates at New York's Famous Door on 52nd street, Woody knew the band was on its way.

Events showed that what makes a hit record does not necessarily make a band however, and soon the 'Blues' policy had to go. After various attempts to find a style, the band emerged again in 1943 with what was subsequently christened The First Herd. This was the band that was swung along by a splendid rhythm section containing Dave Tough on drums, Chubby Jackson on bass, Billy Bauer on guitar, and Ralph Burns (who was doing a number of Ellington-inspired arrangements) on piano. Neal Hefti was on trumpet and was also starting to contribute scores to the library, and also in the band were such now established names (though then barely known) as tenor saxist Flip Phillips, altoist Pete Mondello, trombonist Bill Harris, trumpeter Pete Condoli, and a girl called Marjie Hyams who played excellent vibraphone, and later became a star member of the George Shearing quartet. This was the band that produced such records as *Caldonia* and *Apple Honey*.

But success, like failure, breeds its own problems, and by 1946 a shocked profession read in its trade press that Woody was disbanding. *Metronome* headlined its story: 'Obituary in Rhythm.' The cause was simple. Everyone was telling Herman what he ought to do, from ballroom managers to recording managers to agents to radio producers. And they were all saying the same thing: 'If you want to stay on top you've got to become more commercial.' They were wrong, and the limitations that Woody, in following their advice, began to impose on his bright, young, creative musicians simply created a band of disgruntled prima donnas.

But Herman could not rest. In 1948 he launched the Second Herd, the one with Stan Getz and Zoot Sims that produced *The Four Brothers*. A third and then a fourth Herd followed. By the mid sixties goodness knows what number Herd was in existence, because by then Woody, unlike so many other stars of the Swing era, was not only still surviving, but in constant demand. But he learned one thing from Benny Goodman. The way to survive was to form a band only for special occasions: a special recording session, or some special national or international tour. And something Woody never lost was his talent for finding good, keen, new, young musicians. Consequently when he arrived on his most recent European tour with Herd the Umpteenth, people were still saying: 'What a fantastic band.'

There remains one more white band whose story we must tell, and I have left it till last because it is the band which, more than any other, brings most nostalgia to most people—the feeling of 'That's what it was all about'. Of course I mean Glenn Miller. We referred to him earlier when we described the band he put together for Ray Noble. And it was while he was playing in that band in 1937 that Miller decided to take the plunge. I think he figured that he'd played for so many leaders, and seen them make so many mistakes, that there couldn't be many left for him to make if he was sensible (which he was), efficient and a good organizer (which he was), and understood musicians (which he did, though some will disagree). Also, he

Woody Herman and the Herd in the film *Winter Time*

was a good arranger in his own right. To quote George Simon and his book *The Big Bands* yet again: 'The entire career of the Glenn Miller band lasted just eight years. The last six were glorious; the first two were horrendous.'

The band started rehearsals in March. Later that same month they had their first record session. Glenn was dissatisfied and kept on rehearsing, overhauling and changing the band. In June they played their first major engagement at the Hotel Roosevelt in New Orleans, followed by others in Dallas and Minneapolis. The customers were unenthusiastic and Miller was still dissatisfied. Things went from bad to worse, and at one point he disbanded completely.

Glenn Miller

Some six months later he reassembled a new band on which, you might say, he had decided to stake his all. One of his troubles up to that point had been that he couldn't afford to hire the musicians he really wanted, to play the music he had in mind. He claimed that the 'clarinet on top of five saxes sound', that distinctive Miller trademark, had been invented accidentally. It had happened when, having done an arrangement for Ray Noble, he found that a deputy trumpet player couldn't play the top part he had written. He gave it to clarinettist Johnny Mince instead, and that became 'The Miller Sound'. But it needed a musician of outstanding ability to get it just right. At one point he had Irving Fazola in the band, a musician who could certainly make the right sound, but Miller couldn't afford his salary. Then he came upon Wilbur Schwartz, and at last the problem was solved. Tex Beneke joined on tenor, and Ray Eberle (brother of Jimmy Dorsey's Bob Eberly) came in to sing, as did Marion Hutton (sister of Betty).

Then came the breakthrough. No one can explain it. Miller was still dissatisfied with the band, the bookings were bad, the records they were making not much better. Suddenly a call to play a summer season at the famous Glen Island Casino. Hearing of this in advance, Frank Dailey, who owned that other famous band spot, The Meadowbrook, came up with an offer of an engagement prior to the Casino opening. Miller leapt at the chance, because the bands at The Meadowbrook got a guarantee of 10 broadcasts per week. He brought Maurice Purtill into the band on drums, Bill Finegan (of Sauter/Finegan) started to do some of the band's arrangements, and by the time the Casino opening date arrived the band was really beginning to sound like something.

So, as the Palomar had been to Benny Goodman, the Glen Island Casino was to be to Glenn Miller. By the time they reached it, he had upped the brass section to four trumpets and four trombones—one of the first bands ever to do so—and the guaranteed broadcasting that came with the Casino job, as it had done at the Meadowbrook, finally meant that the band was on its way. However, it still hadn't got a hit record. The wait was not long. While still with Ray Noble, Miller had written a song called *Now I Lay Me Down to Weep*. This, with new lyrics, and re-titled *Moonlight Serenade*, became the band's theme tune and was issued as a record. It was followed in a matter of weeks by their recording of Bill Finegan's arrangement of *Little Brown Jug*, and you could say that the rest became history.

The arrival of the Swing era caught most of the black Big Bands on the wrong foot. It was totally unexpected, hit them with the speed of a comet, and in any case what was so new about those Fletcher Henderson arrangements that Benny Goodman was playing so successfully? They'd failed for Fletcher's own band, hadn't they? There were exceptions. Ellington sailed regally on. Count Basie jumped on the wagon facing the right way and became an overnight success (well, almost). And Lionel Hampton, being of a later generation and a Goodman employee anyway, was in a position to observe, and when he judged the time right, to cash in. But for a number of fine bands it was the beginning of the end.

Chick Webb, who might have made it, unfortunately died in 1939. Ella Fitzgerald nominally took over the band, but it soon became obvious that solo singing was more her 'thing' than band-leading, and that was that. Perhaps the biggest disappointment of all for the fans was the gradual decline and fall of the Jimmie Lunceford Band. He had taken over the residency at the Cotton Club from Ellington, Sy Oliver had joined on trumpet and started doing a whole string of successful arrangements for the library (*For Dancers Only*, *My Blue Heaven*, and *Four or Five Times* are three stand-outs), and by 1937 it was probably the most sought after of all the black bands for one-night stand dates. Oliver left to join Tommy Dorsey in 1939 but his scores were still played, and in any event Lunceford had other good arrangers available, notably Edwin Wilcox. Indeed at a mammoth band concert at New York's Manhattan Center in 1940 it was the Lunceford band that managed to up-stage everybody on a bill that included the Goodman, Miller, Basie and Brown bands, to say nothing of Lombardo, Sammy Kaye, and a number of others who appeared between 8 pm and 4 am. But some-how nothing seemed to go quite right, and the band began to get somewhat ragged and dispirited. Sy Oliver, whose main reason for leaving was that he was fed up with the never ending one-night stands, was later quoted as saying that it was these that finally caused the band's downfall. Lunceford had many good musicians, but one by one they all got sick of touring. The end finally came in 1947 with Jimmie's death following a heart attack.

The early years of the Duke Ellington band have already been outlined, and the highlights of this remarkable man's career are given in our A–Z. But one must pause to remark that if ever a bandleader succeeded by continuing to 'do his own thing' unaffected by the changing scene around him, Duke was that man. It was in 1940 that arranger Billy Strayhorn joined him and soon became, next to the master himself, the single most important influence on the band's music. The war years left their mark

Jimmie Lunceford and his Orchestra, 1936

on the Ellington personnel as indeed they did on every Big Band. But curiously they affected Duke less, and many critics cite the early forties as a peak period in the band's history. Certainly it was the time when perhaps they swung even more solidly than at any other. It was the period that produced records like *Jack The Bear*, *Cotton Tail*, *Just a-sittin' and a-rockin'*, *Perdido*, *C Jam Blues* and *Take The 'A' Train* to name but a few.

Then there was the 1943 Carnegie Hall concert to which we have already referred. This conferred upon the band a kind of social status and acceptance they do not seem to have fully possessed before. It was the occasion of course of the first performance of Duke's *Black Brown and Beige* Suite, up to that point his most prestigious work. And it was a 'work', lasting some 45 minutes, and not a series of popular songs. One cannot but wonder if the reaction of audience and critics did not contribute to the newly found acceptance!

It is certainly a fact that from then on the band was welcomed at many of the venues that had previously refused to book them, and their list of concert engagements expanded enormously. From the post war years through to his death in 1974 at the age of 71, Ellington and his band were rivalled only by Louis Armstrong as 'Ambassadors' of Jazz and Big Band music in almost every country in both the Western and Eastern worlds. He had been among the first to start, and he stayed the course continuously longer than anyone else. And in spite of his ever increasing involvement in prestigious events (his 'sacred' concerts in Cathedrals everywhere became a byword during the sixties and seventies), he never neglected the loyal and often ageing fans who rode the course with him. At an Ellington concert you could count on hearing some of your favourites, whether they be *Creole Love Call* or *Take The 'A' Train*, even though you might also find yourself being introduced for the first time to a major new work such as *David Danced before the Lord with all his Might*. Back in 1953 the late critic Ralph Gleason had written in the *San Francisco Chronicle*: 'I would like to predict that a quarter of a century hence Duke's music will be studied in the schools, and critics will grant him his true place beside the great composers of this century.' Not quite yet, Mr. Gleason. But give a conservative world time!

There are two other important black bands we have not touched on. Lionel Hampton left it until 1940 before he quit his safe seat as a star performer in the Benny Goodman band to have a go on his own. In a remarkably short space of time he had welded together a swinging, jubilant, somewhat frenetic outfit that seemed very much to reflect its leader's mercurial personality. With a hit record, *Flyin' Home* in 1943, they were soon set on the course for fame, and indeed they seemed to survive the general decline of the big band scene of the late forties better than most. By 1953 they had already undertaken many overseas tours including Australia, Japan, Europe, Africa and the Middle East, though curiously it was 1969 before they appeared in London. Hamp's bands have always been breeding grounds for musicians who were later to become well known in their own right: Charlie Mingus, Quincy Jones, Illinois Jacquet, Joe Newman, Cat Anderson, as well as singers Joe Williams and Dinah Washington, are just a few.

And of course, there is still the remarkable William 'Count' Basie. He was with Bennie Moten when the latter died in 1935, and after taking over for a spell, his bandleading career proper began with the

Barons of Rhythm at the Reno Club in Kansas City in 1936. Here they were heard by John Hammond, one of the unsung backroom men of Jazz who had already done so much to further Benny Goodman's career. He persuaded the big agency MCA to sign them up, and they were given opportunities at a string of good locations from the Grand Terrace in Chicago to the Roseland Ballroom in New York. Success was not all that quick to come however. George T. Simon, reviewing the band for *Metronome* in 1937 wrote: 'True, the band does swing, but that sax section is so invariably out of tune. And if you think that sax section is out of tune, catch the brass!'

However, by 1938 they had obtained a residency at Harlem's Savoy Ballroom, and this was followed by a booking at that Jazz mecca, the Famous Door. By now the band, which had already collected

Count Basie

Buck Clayton, Lester Young, Herschel Evans, Jo Jones and Walter Page along the way, was boosted by the addition of such stalwarts as Freddy Green, Harry Edison, Ed Lewis, Benny Morton, Dicky Wells and blues singer Jimmy Rushing. The only loss was that they had had a virtually unknown Billie Holiday as their girl singer, and she now left to join Artie Shaw. In any event they could never have recorded together because Basie was signed to Decca and Billie had just been signed by Brunswick. Later the Count recalled: 'She was our first girl vocalist and she was beautiful to work with. I used to be just as thrilled to hear her as the audience was.' Helen Humes, a fine singer, took her place. But there was only one 'Lady Day'.

By the time of the Famous Door date not only was the band really beginning to take shape, but its Decca records were beginning to catch on. This was the period of their most famous hit, their theme song *One O'Clock Jump*, as well as *Sent For You Yesterday*, *Jumpin' At The Woodside*, *Blue and Sentimental*, and *Every Tub*. And of course Basie now had the biggest single asset he ever had in that great rhythm section —himself on piano, Freddie Green on guitar, Walter Page on bass, and Jo Jones on drums. Faithful Freddie Green remained with him to help lay down the beat, but Jo Jones left soon after the war and Walter Page in 1949. But always their successors seem to have been able to slip swiftly into the production of that distinctive 'Basie beat'— emulated by many but never successfully.

Unlike Lionel Hampton, the decline of the late forties did affect the Count. In fact he was forced to disband in 1950, and for quite a few years cut back to a sextet. However he fought back, assembled another Big Band, and by the mid fifties was embarked on successful tours of Europe, especially

Scandinavia, making his British début in 1957. This come-back was greatly aided by support from Frank Sinatra who booked the band to accompany him on many of his prestigious concerts, including a momentous occasion at London's Royal Festival Hall in 1970, and lucrative bookings in Las Vegas. Bill Basie is still active with the same kind of swinging outfit in 1977, but like other wise leaders of his generation, he now only puts a band together for those special occasions that can pay the kind of money it takes, to get the kind of musicians it takes, to play that 'Basie beat'.

Several times in our story we have referred to that magic date in August 1935 when Benny Goodman and his Band gave birth to Swing. We have also indicated that the demise of Big Band music began in earnest just 11 years later when, in 1946 within a space of weeks, no fewer than eight of the world's top bands broke up. If George T. Simon will permit me yet another quote from his book *The Big Bands*—'For a few years the bands hung on, but slowly more and more began to hang up their horns for good, and the world that was once theirs now became the property of a group of their most illustrious graduates—the singers!' We will examine the reasons for that decline, and see the effect it had on what remains of the Big Band scene today, but first a few words about the war years on both sides of the Atlantic, and about the bands that they produced.

Unusually, Britain was ahead of America in the formation of what might loosely be called the Service bands. As early as 1939 Sir Walford Davies, Master of the King's Musick, let it be known that if some of London's leading dance musicians happened to join the RAF together, he would see to it that their talents were not wasted! So it was that the RAF Dance

The Squadronaires. Ronnie Aldrich fourth from left, back

Orchestra, later to become world famous as the Squadronaires, was formed. Amongst its initial personnel were Tommy McQuater among the trumpets, George Chisholm on trombone, Andy McDevitt and Harry Lewis (Vera Lynn's husband) among the saxes, Ronnie Aldrich on piano, Sid Colin on guitar, and Jock Cummings on drums. Out front as leader it had Jimmy Miller, soon to be promoted to Sergeant.

Much of its music was loosely based on the Big Band Dixieland style of the Bob Crosby Orchestra, and this brought instant success via broadcasts and records. In 1941 the radio reporter of the *Melody Maker* enthused: '. . . the greatest dance band performance that has ever been broadcast this side of the Atlantic.' Much credit must go to the inspired

arrangements of George Chisholm and Ronnie Aldrich, and to such never to be forgotten features as the unison trombone duets by George and Eric Breeze. When the war ended the band still had 12 of its original members (Harry Lewis had been invalided out in 1943), the brass had gone up from 4 to 5, and there was a full-blooded saxophone team that now included Cliff Townshend and Monty Levy.

When the band were finally all demobbed they decided to stay together on a co-operative basis (again not unlike the Bob Crosby Orchestra), and before long Ronnie Aldrich took over the musical direction from Jimmy Miller. Until the band finally broke up in the mid sixties it still retained some of its founder members. And even though it sometimes changed its musical policy (once with near disastrous results when it decided to have a go at Rock 'n

Roll before anybody had heard of Bill Haley), it remains *the* important band of the forties and fifties.

But Britain had other good Service bands. There was the Skyrockets (officially the No. 1 Balloon Centre Dance Orchestra) led by Paul Fenhoulet, a band which also stayed together after the war and perhaps reached its greatest popularity when it became the pit orchestra at the London Palladium. Here throughout the fifties and sixties the world's greatest variety and musical acts were to be seen and heard, and the Skyrockets' accompanying contributions were universally praised. The Army had the Blue Rockets of the Royal Ordnance Corps, led in its early days by the late Eric Robinson of *Melodies for You* fame. And the Royal Navy had the Blue Mariners led by George Crowe, and containing among others a man who was perhaps as great a performer on his alto sax as George Chisholm was on his trombone—the late Freddie Gardner.

But if for once Britain was first in the field in setting up the Service bands, America, as might be expected, scooped the pool in size and glamour. In 1942 Glenn Miller gave up his civilian band to join the Army. They gave him the rank of Captain, and the pick of musicians was to be his. It must have been quite a decision for him to take. He was too old to be drafted, and since that initial success at the Glen Island Casino the world had latched onto a stack of sensationally popular recordings, and the band simply could not fulfil all the personal appearances it was offered throughout the States. The mere mention of such titles as *Tuxedo Junction*, *Pennsylvania 65000* (Jerry Gray's first big hit as Miller's new arranger), *String of Pearls*, *Chattanooga Choo-Choo*, *At Last* and *Perfidia* are enough to arouse great waves of nostalgia among the elderly, to say nothing of the band's greatest ever hit *In The Mood*.

The Skyrockets in their Palladium days. Leader Woolf Phillips (tmb, centre)

It took Miller and the US Army a long time to get accustomed to each other. Truth to tell, they never really did. The classic example is the oft-quoted battle he had about the use of so-called Jazz arrangements for marching, like *St. Louis Blues March* and *Blues in The Night*. That was a fight he won. Others he lost, such as his continual badgering to get the band more quickly into the real areas of war. But by 1943 the Army Air Force Band was well under way, and already beginning to contain some of those legendary names with which we were all soon to become so familiar—Ray McKinley on drums, Zeke Zarchy and Bernie Privin among the trumpets, Mel Powell on piano, Trigger Alpert on bass, Carmen Maestren on guitar, Peanuts Hucko on clarinet and alto. And of course many more who joined later when the AAF band was enlarged by a

Glenn Miller conducting the American Band of the AEF in 1944

full sized symphonic string section, french horns, and extra percussion, to become the American Band of the AEF (Allied Expeditionary Force). Glenn of course collected promotion to the rank of Major along the way!

The AEF band came to Britain early in 1944, giving BBC broadcasts and appearing at special troop concerts. Frequently they were joined by stars from both countries—Bing Crosby and Anne Shelton were but two.

Then came the order: 'Your next posting is Paris.' And it was all over. In December 1944 Miller took off in a small plane for France to make arrangements for the band's arrival a few days later. Neither he nor the plane were ever seen or heard of again. The AEF orchestra played on under Jerry Gray and Ray McKinley until their time came to be demobbed. After the war Glenn's widow Helen, and the trustees of the Miller estate, gave their blessing to a variety of 'Glenn Miller Bands led by . . .' including Tex Beneke and Buddy de Franco. But perhaps the most remarkable tribute to this remarkable man and his music is that in London, at The Royal Albert Hall in December 1975, an almost unknown British band of unashamed Miller-style copyists calling themselves The Million Airs could, augmented by a string section and presented by broadcaster Alan Dell, sell-out those 3,000 plus Albert Hall seats for a Miller/AEF Memorial Concert. We shall return to the subject of nostalgia for the great days of the Big Bands in the closing section of this history.

Pre-eminent though the American Band of the AEF was, neither Britain nor indeed Canada trailed behind this particular Service bandwagon. Britain created a similarly large orchestra called, not surprisingly, the British Band of the AEF. This

George
Melachrino

was directed by George Melachrino, a fine musician who had started his career in the twenties playing saxophone and violin as well as singing with the Savoy Orpheans, and who had gone on to become the leader of one of the country's most popular light music orchestras. He was an ideal man for the job, having a good grounding in all the various kinds of music the orchestra was required to play as well as being a first class arranger and a talented composer (his *Winter Sunshine* will be well remembered). The British brass hats could not, of course, quite bring themselves actually to commission a musician. So throughout the war George had to get by as Regimental Sergeant Major George Melachrino (RSM for short). The Canadians were less conservative, and were quite happy to make their fine pianist, arranger and composer Captain Bob Farnon when they appointed him Director of the

Canadian Band of the AEF. There was one short period towards the end of 1944 when all three of the AEF Orchestras were stationed in England, and broadcasting regularly via the BBC.

Before leaving the war years we must mention one other British name band that sprang to prominence at that time. Albert McCarthy in his book: *The Dance Band Era* says: 'There is no doubt that to a generation that missed the halcyon dance band era of the thirties, and grew up during the early forties, Geraldo occupies much the same niche in Britain as does Glenn Miller in the United States.' An overstatement I would think, but of 'Gerry's popularity there can be no doubt. Geraldo (real name Gerald Bright) first entered the London band scene in the twenties. But his break came in the early thirties when he moved into the Savoy Hotel Ballroom with Geraldo's Gaucho Tango Band. Successful for many years in this area of music, in the late thirties Gerry started moving towards the Big Bands culminating in 1939 with a good band that included such names as Harry Hayes, Andy McDevitt and George Evans (who did many of the band's best arrangements) among the saxes.

In the early days of the war he was appointed Director of the Band Division of ENSA, supplying numerous bands in addition to his own and undertaking several tours of the various battle zones. His own particular band, which was of course ENSA's star performer, continued to grow in musical strength, acquiring such additional names as trumpeter Leslie 'Jiver' Hutchinson, guitarist Ivor Mairants, pianist Norman Stenfalt, clarinettist Nat Temple, trombonist Laddie Busby and alto saxophonist Wally Stott; there were also accomplished singers: Dorothy Carless, Doreen Villiers, Beryl Davis and Len Camber among them.

Geraldo, 1933

Beryl Davis
about 1945

Plenty of broadcasting and recording meant that by 1945 Geraldo's orchestra was certainly a major force both in Europe and the UK. His popularity continued through the early fifties, but he gradually fell a victim to the general demise of the Big Bands, and he concentrated more and more on his agency and artists booking business, making only occasional concert appearances until his death in 1975. Among the records he left behind many will be affectionately remembered, especially perhaps *Soft Shoe Shuffle*, '*T'is Autumn* and Dorothy Carless's big hits, *Ragtime Cowboy Joe* and *That Lovely Weekend*.

It is curious to reflect that until 1939 Britain didn't really have a big band in the American Swing band sense of the word, though Joe Loss was trying hard. The war seemed to create them however, for another was born towards the end, Ted Heath and His Music, perhaps Britain's greatest contribution of all to the world of the Big Bands. But as his story properly belongs to the fifties we will deal with it when we get there.

We said that the year 1946 marked the beginning of the end for the Big Bands, and that is true. But to understand the causes we must flash back as far as 1942 when the American Federation of Musicians instituted a strike of all its members against the recording companies. The grievance was that the increasing use of juke boxes (which of course played records) in places of entertainment was leading to a decrease in employment for musicians. Whatever the truth of the arguments involved, there is little doubt that this strike was a major contributing factor to the downfall of the bands.

Until that time, with rare exceptions (Bing Crosby was the first to break through the barrier in the mid thirties) a band singer's only credit on a record label was the ubiquitous phrase: 'with vocal

Bing Crosby

refrain by . . .'. Al Bowlly, after many years with Lew Stone and Ray Noble, was beginning to make it on his own when he was killed in an air raid in 1941. Frank Sinatra had to leave Tommy Dorsey to do it, and that was not until the end of 1942.

With musicians unable to record however, the singers came into their own. They were accompanied by just about everything you could think of that didn't belong to the AF of M (organists were doing good business because they were non-members), but mostly they were accompanied by groups of other singers 'oohing and aahing' in the background. It was war time, and people wanted popular songs. And they wanted to hear popular singers interpreting those sentimental lyrics. The singers seized their chance with both tonsils. Out from under the 'with vocal refrain by' tag came

Frank Sinatra of course, but also Perry Como (from Ted Weems), Dick Haymes (Sinatra's replacement with Dorsey), Billy Eckstine (from Earl Hines), Bob Eberly (from Jimmy Dorsey), Ray Eberle (ex Glenn Miller) and many others. Even more important because it was war time were the girls. Goodman's Peggy Lee, Les Brown's Doris Day, Tommy Dorsey's Jo Stafford, Tony Pastor's Rosemary Clooney, Charlie Barnet's Kay Starr—just a few of the 'with vocal refrain by' guys and gals who never looked back, right through the fifties and sixties.

Some record companies found themselves forced to negotiate after the strike had been on a year. Other larger companies hung on till the end of 1944. Like the joint MU/AF of M ban on the exchange of musicians in the thirties, there is no doubt at all that the recording strike did more harm than good to those very musicians it was designed to

Perry Como

help. For when the musicians were able to get back into the recording studios, the record companies were more interested in utilizing their services as accompanying units for their newly found stars, the singers, than they were in recreating the sounds of the Big Bands *per se*.

Many leading musicians were still in the armed forces of course, but when they did come back home they found little to attract them into joining once again the constant round of touring and one-night stands. If they lived near the big studio centres, New York, Los Angeles, Chicago (or London), there was lucrative work to be had as session men in the recording or broadcasting or film studios. Later television virtually supplanted films.

Rosemary
Clooney

The booking agencies, realizing that now singers were a greater attraction to the public than bands, were naturally not offering the best dates, and the second best dates didn't pay enough money to enable a bandleader to keep good men on his payroll, for musicians' salaries were now way up above 1939 standards. With post-war recession setting in all round, there was no way the big hotels and ballrooms could consistently pay the kind of money now demanded by a good band. So, although a number of bands struggled on through the fifties and even into the sixties, those few weeks in 1946 which saw the breakup of the Goodman, Herman, Dorsey, James and Brown bands, among others, really were the beginning of the end.

There are however two success stories of the fifties: Stan Kenton in America and Ted Heath in Britain. And a greater contrast in both men and music you could not wish to meet. Stan Kenton has been labelled as the father of 'progressive Jazz'—which Ted Heath was frequently heard to refer to as 'starvation music'.

You could most accurately describe Ted's as a jazz-orientated, hard swinging band, a kind of amalgam perhaps of Goodman, Herman and Lunceford, yet with arrangements that owed little to any of these, a library with a high proportion of original compositions, and with a great commercial vocal team—Lita Roza, Dennis Lotis, Dickie Valentine, and singing compere Paul Carpenter (lately from Bob Farnon's Canadian AEF Band). Ted started tentatively with broadcasting in 1944, but did not form his first real band until 1945. By 1947/48 its broadcasts, its records and its series of Sunday night Swing Sessions at the London Palladium were fast making it into a legend in its own time.

Kenton on the other hand started his first band in 1941. He was on a 'progressive' course from the start. George Simon faulted the band in an early review in *Metronome* for 'continual blasting'. Another critic, Barry Ulanov, said: 'But there's no reason why so formidable an organization must always sound like a moving man grunting under the weight of a concert grand.' Eddie Condon in his *Treasury of Jazz* said: 'music of his school, in my opinion, ought only to be played close to elephants and listened to only by clowns.' None of this deterred Stan who stayed rigidly in his progressive groove, and by 1943 his recordings of *Artistry in Rhythm* and *Eager Beaver* were attracting considerable attention (some five or six years later Jack Jackson, by then England's top disc jockey, made *Eager Beaver* into a minor UK hit by continually playing it on his Saturday night record show).

Stan Kenton has one thing in common with Woody Herman—a knack of finding new, young, talented musicians. His band became a positive breeding ground—Eddie Safranski, Shelley Manne, Buddy Childers, Chico Alvarez, Kai Winding, Boots Musilli, Bob Cooper, and Pete Rugulo (who contributed enormously to the arranging side) were just a few. And a cute blonde called June Christy came out from of nowhere and turned into a very good singer indeed with such titles as *Willow Weep For Me*, *Tampico* and *Just a-sittin' and a-rockin'*. By the fifties, when the bands were really fading away, not so Stan Kenton. He abandoned ballrooms for concerts. His music, he said, had never been right for dancing anyway. By the sixties, with Rock 'n' Roll really upon us, Kenton had become the darling of the university campuses. And through into the seventies he still does concert tours, such as his European tour in 1977.

Above: Stan Kenton and June Christy

Left: Anne Shelton with the comedian Ronnie Shiner and Dom Bernhard (the Padre) broadcasting to the forces in 1941

Meanwhile across the Atlantic eastwards, Ted Heath was going from strength to strength in a completely different direction. In England after the war, when the big time pre-war bandleaders started to try and put together the pieces again, they faced many of the same problems as their American counterparts, and some others as well. Here too, the singers were 'making it big'. The public wanted to see as well as hear Vera Lynn, Anne Shelton, Sam Browne and Sam Costa. Later it was to be Joan Regan and Alma Cogan, Dickie Valentine and David Whitfield. The recession and the lack of money was even greater than in America. MU rates went up, attendances at ballrooms began going down.

Managements began cutting the size of their bands—an 18 piece went down to 14, soon to 12, then to an octet. The West End hotels found they didn't need Bert Ambrose and Lew Stone any more. The customers, such as they were, came for less well publicized but quite efficient if dull bands, who were

Vera Lynn

Dickie
Valentine,

perfectly capable of churning out hour after hour of
ceaseless 'um-ching, um-ching', which seemed to be
all the customers wanted. Lew Stone conducted in
a theatre pit; Jack Hylton had become a famous
impresario; Jack Jackson the country's leading disc
jockey; Ambrose was traipsing round the country
with an inferior band on a series of one-night stands
he would not even have contemplated in 1939.

By the fifties they had all faded from the band
scene, and apart from The Squadronaires and
Geraldo, only Ted Heath with his all-star personnel
(Kenny Baker, Dave Wilkins, Stan Roderick, Harry
Roche, Laddie Busby, Les Gilbert, Reg Owen,
Johnny Gray, Henry McKenzie and Jack Parnell
were just some of his early performers), was successful with rounds of concerts, dances, broadcasting and
recording dates. In retrospect however, perhaps

Ted Heath and his Music

Ted's greatest claim to fame is one which is only partly musical. In 1955 he became the first British band to break through the infamous MU/AF of M interchange ban which had been in existence since the mid thirties. He embarked on the first of many highly successful tours of the States, and through to his death in 1969 Ted Heath and His Music continued to rate among the top four big bands in the world. Possibly Ellington, Basie and Herman were his only rivals.

As the singers had taken over in the fifties, so by the sixties the bands had been totally replaced as major attractions, in the states by Rock 'n' Roll (Bill Haley and the Comets started all that in the middle fifties), and in England by that curiosity called the Trad Boom. This also started in the fifties with the revival of interest in traditional Jazz culminating in the enormous success of 'The Three B's—Chris Barber, Kenny Ball, and Acker Bilk. Economics again played a large part in all of this. The average Rock 'n' Roll group would be about five to seven musicians strong, the average Trad band seven or eight. Who needed to pay for a band of some 18 musicians plus a team of singers, if a five to eight piece group would fill a theatre or a ballroom just as easily?

And one must not finally close the coffin lid without drawing a parallel between the fate of Swing and the fate of Jazz. As Modern Jazz took over from Traditional Jazz so the popularity of the medium with the public at large went into a decline. There are many critics who, while agreeing on the important roles played both by the singers and by the economic stringencies of the time, see the final nail in the lid as the 'progressive' influence of Stan Kenton and those who followed him. Ted Heath, as we have said, described it as 'starvation music', yet Kenton made a success out of it. But those who followed him on both sides of the Atlantic failed miserably. In America Boyd Raeburn and Billy Eckstine tried, but despite much praise for their efforts from both musicians and fans they couldn't pull it off. In England Vic Lewis and Tommy Sampson met with the same fate. John Dankworth tried bravely with various compromises to keep his head above water, but in the end he too had to give up.

And so to the present. In America some of the surviving great names occasionally emerge for special tours or performances—Goodman, Herman, Basie, James and Kenton are, I suppose, the leading lights in this category. In Britain a curious thing has happened. It all started in the late sixties when a young trumpet player called Syd Lawrence suddenly decided to form a band with the policy of playing note-for-note copies of Glenn Miller's records. The result—almost instant success. Lawrence has kept this band together through the seventies, and has now broadened his policy to include copies of many other great bands like Barnet, Goodman, Shaw and Tommy Dorsey. His records have become big sellers, and apart from successful personal appearances up and down the country, he seems to be able to sell-out his concerts at London's Royal Festival or Royal Albert Halls almost whenever he wants to. And Lawrence has been followed by another band of copycats to whom we have already referred briefly, The Million Airs, though their success, good as they were, seems at the time of writing to have been short-lived.

Finally and most astonishingly of all there has been that brave but bizarre revival, The New Paul Whiteman Orchestra. Formed for the Camden Jazz Festival in London in 1974, they survived

Syd Lawrence conducting the brass section of his orchestra

miraculously for about two years. Some 28 of Britain's top session musicians gave their minds and efforts to this project, the brainchild of one American then resident in England, journalist and cornet player Richard Sudhalter. Richard, author of the definitive biography of the great trumpeter Bix Beiderbecke, had come across the Paul Whiteman library during his research. He obtained permission from the trustees of the Whiteman estate to use the name and the music, and lo and behold, to quote from the sleeve note of their first record: 'The New Paul Whiteman Orchestra, 28 tuxedos strong, filed onto stage at London's Roundhouse to perform an evening of 50 year old popular music. The result was 'sheer magic.'

Where will it all end, one asks oneself? In the US there is some evidence that nostalgia is popular, but to nothing like the extent that has happened in the UK. For this tribute must be paid to broadcaster Alan Dell for his two long-running programmes on BBC Radio 2, *The Dance Band Days*, which revives the great British dance bands, and *The Big Band Sound*, which features the best of the American Swingers from Paul Whiteman to Stan Kenton. Fans of this kind of music owe much to Alan Dell.

As a postscript, it would be wrong to close without a look at the Big Band scene in the rest of Europe, outside Britain. There is not a lot to report, certainly in the early years. As in the UK, no real attempts were made to copy America's Swing era, and so until recently the remaining European contribution has been small. The main dance bands of the thirties with some pretensions to Swing were Ray Ventura's from France, Kai Ewans' from Denmark, and The Ramblers from Holland. Of these, the most interesting were The Ramblers. Coleman Hawkins, then America's top Jazz tenor man, played with them on an extended tour in 1935, and some excellent records were made to testify to it, including sessions where they were also joined by Britain's George Chisholm and America's Benny Carter. Ray Ventura's early band was, like Jack Hylton's, Whiteman based. He modernized it a good deal in the late thirties, and indeed visited Britain in 1931, 1938 and 1946, by which time it had something of the showband performance about it. Kai Ewans achieved considerable success in the thirties because, like The Ramblers, his band was somewhat Jazz orientated. Indeed it was frequently the accompanying unit for such visiting Americans as Adelaide Hall and Benny Carter.

Belgium produced a good band led by Fud Candrix, and although Germany banned 'decadent

James Last

Bert Kaempfert

western Swing' after the Nazis came to power, the twenties saw a good deal of interest there in dance music. Even after 1933 a series of EMI 78s of Jazz music were still available there. Probably Germany's two best bands were those led by Teddy Stauffer (born in Switzerland, where he returned in 1939), James Kok (born Romanian), and Heinz Wehner and his Telefunken Swing-Orchester. And from Sweden came Thore Ehrling, with a good band that by the late thirties had pretensions to Swing—as demonstrated when Nat Gonella and his brother Bruts recorded with them on a 1939 session.

After the war of course, things changed significantly if somewhat slowly throughout the continent. Perhaps one of the first of the good post-war bands to emerge was that of Germany's Kurt Edelhagen. He was on the scene by the late forties with a Kenton-inspired outfit. In the late fifties Belgium produced the Francis Bay Orchestra which modelled its style on the Big Bands, including Ellington, and, perhaps surprisingly, Ted Heath. But the best known and most successful of all the European bands have clearly been those two stars from Germany, James Last and Bert Kaempfert. These are the only two whose records sell world wide, and that includes America. Both came to prominence in the late fifties, and both are still at the top today. James Last, in addition to his recording activities, undertakes a number of national and international tours. Kaempfert concentrates his activities almost exclusively in the recording studios. Both are to be congratulated on keeping the Big Band flag flying through the seventies. Finally perhaps Britain is currently contributing the most significant development to Big Band music in the form of the National Youth Jazz Orchestra. Indeed this splendid venture has even succeeded in bringing Big Band music to British television. Long may it continue!

MUSICAL ABBREVIATIONS

acc	accordion	**drs**	drums
arr	arranger,	**E gtr**	electric guitar
	arranged by	**F hn**	French horn
alto	alto saxophone	**Fl**	flute
bar	baritone sax	**gtr**	guitar
B bs	brass bass	**perc**	percussion
bjo	banjo	**pno**	piano
bs	double bass	**sax**	saxophone
bs gtr	bass guitar	**sop**	soprano saxophone
bs sax	bass saxophone	**ten**	tenor saxophone
cel	celeste	**tmb**	trombone
clt	clarinet	**tpt**	trumpet
comp	composer,	**tymps**	tympani
	composed by	**vibes**	vibraphone
cor	cornet	**vln**	violin
dir	musical director	**voc**	vocal

Note: because of limitations of space it has been possible to include only the briefest biographical details of many of the bandleaders and personalities involved in this book. For further details readers should consult some of the excellent books listed in the Bibliography.

THE ARRANGERS

Burns, Ralph Started learning piano aged 7,
later studying at the New England Conservatory.
Joined Charlie Barnet's band in New York, 1940,
then to Red Norvo 1943, and to Woody Herman
1944 (at the same time as Neal Hefti). It was here
that his arranging career really began, and he has
retained the strongest links with Herman ever since,
although for many years he has been active in
writing for Benny Goodman, films, TV etc. In the
Herman band he was part of one of its strongest
rhythm sections when he was on piano in the company of Dave Tough (drs), Chubby Jackson (bs)
and Billy Bauer (gtr). Among his famous originals
for Woody are *Bijou* (which featured Bill Harris,
trombone); and *Lady McGowan's Dream*. Also of
course *Summer Sequence*, the latter part of which
formed the basis for the later *Early Autumn*. *Rhapsody
in Wood* was another feature he wrote for the band.
His writing has always reflected his admiration for
the work of Duke Ellington, while his piano work
especially with the Woodchoppers small groups has
usually proved interesting. In other areas he has
written wide-ranging works such as *Introspection*
(1946) and the eight part *Free Forms* (1951) designed
for the solo alto of Lee Konitz.

Camarata, Salvatore 'Toots' or 'Tutti' A trumpet
player who began to make a name as an arranger
when playing in Charlie Barnet's first band (1933).
Moved to Jimmy Dorsey when the latter formed his
Big Band in 1935, and had his first really major hits

with his scores of the Bob Eberly/Helen O'Connell duets *Green Eyes*, *Amapola*, *Yours* and *Tangerine* (1941). He also contributed excellent arrangements for Paul Whiteman's attempt to re-shape his band in the early 1940s. From about that time Camarata gave up playing to concentrate on full time arranging, and has always been regarded as one of America's top musicians in this field.

Challis, William H. 'Bill'   Self-taught pianist who later took up C melody sax and arranging. Big break: joining Jean Goldkette as staff arranger (1926). Moved to Paul Whiteman until 1930 and was responsible for many of the now famous Whiteman scores that featured Bix Beiderbecke and Frank Trumbauer solos. From then on became freelance contributing to the bands of Fletcher Henderson, the Dorsey Brothers, The Casa Loma Orchestra etc. For a long time specialized in radio work; his later work was more directed to commercial requirements than to the Big Band scene.

Conniff, Ray   Trombonist who started his arranging career with Bunny Berigan's band 1937–39. From there he went to Artie Shaw, for whom he made some splendid arrangements, and to whom he returned briefly in 1944. Also either played with or contributed scores to Bob Crosby, Harry James etc. Later became a staff musician/arranger for ABC New York. 1954 gave up playing to concentrate on arranging, and by mid 1950s had his own band and singers. Since then he has gone from success to success, concentrating mainly on his singers.

Finegan, William 'Bill'   Really sprang into the limelight when he joined Glenn Miller in 1939. He was responsible for the arrangement of *Little Brown*

Jug, one of the band's earliest hits. In 1943, with the Miller band broken up, he brought new life to the Tommy Dorsey band during one of its difficult periods. He also worked for Horace Heidt and a number of other leaders. But probably his most spectacular contribution to the Big Bands was teaming up in 1952 with Eddie Sauter to form the Sauter/Finegan Orchestra. This marvellous outfit with its innovatory sounds will probably be best remembered for its recordings of *Doodletown Fifers* and *Midnight Sleighride*. Unfortunately it was too sophisticated for the public taste, and both arrangers went back to freelance activities.

Gifford, Harold Eugene 'Gene' Guitarist who joined the Casa Loma Orchestra in 1929, took up arranging, and largely guided the band to fame in the 1930s. *White Jazz, Black Jazz, Blue Jazz, Maniac's Ball*, and *Casa Loma Stomp* will recall the sound. Left the band in 1935 to concentrate on freelance arranging. Also did a spell as staff arranger for station WWL New Orleans in 1945. Returned to Glen Gray (Casa Loma leader) 1948–49, but the band broke up in 1950, and while Gifford continued arranging for other leaders for many years, he gradually switched to his other love and became a full time radio engineer and audio consultant.

Gray, Jerry Started out playing violin and accordion, joining Artie Shaw during his string quartet period of 1936–37. Left the band but rejoined later as arranger and was responsible for their big hit *Begin The Beguine*. When Shaw's band suffered one of its many break-ups (1939) Gray switched to Glenn Miller where he was soon responsible for a string of hits, one of the first being *Pennsylvania 6500*. He stayed with Glenn throughout, joining up with him in 1943, and had a big hand together with Miller and Ray McKinley in the marching *St. Louis Blues* and *Blues in The Night* scores for the Army Air Force band. After Miller's death in 1944, Gray shared the leadership of the AEF Band with Ray McKinley. After the war he formed a band of his own, probably the best of the Miller copyist outfits. After a while however he gave it up and went to live on the West Coast, concentrating on film and TV work.

Hefti, Neal   Trumpet player who started arranging in 1941, springing to prominence as a member of the bands of Charlie Barnet and Bobby Byrne. 1942 started writing for Earl Hines Big Band, later moving to Hollywood with Charlie Spivak. In 1944 he joined the Woody Herman band at the same time as Ralph Burns. His arrangements soon became outstanding, and included *The Good Earth* and *Wild Root* (in honour of the company which sponsored the band's weekly radio programme). Married Woody's singer Frances Wayne 1945, and left band to join first Charlie Ventura then Harry James. During the 1950s he more or less gave up playing to concentrate on writing, contributing such famous numbers as *Little Pony, L'il Darlin'* and *The Kid From Red Bank* to the Count Basie library. Has occasionally led Big Bands of his own, but has concentrated more and more on writing in the popular music field, where his work for TV, particularly his writing for singers, has been outstanding.

May, William E. 'Billy'   A trumpet player who had played with many bands before joining Charlie Barnet in 1939 and doing some of the band's best arrangements, including *Wings Over Manhattan*. Left to join Glenn Miller (1940–41), then with Les

Brown (1942) and Alvino Rey (1943). Moved to California and did arranging and conducting for radio shows. Started recording for Capitol 1951 as a studio band, and the success of these records led him to form a regular band which he had until 1953 when he returned to freelance arranging and the band was taken over by Sam Donahue. He did and continues to do many Hollywood films and TV shows and was Musical Director of the Time–Life *Swing Era* re-creation record series (*see* Discography).

Mundy, James 'Jimmy' In his early days played tenor sax in Chicago with such bands as Erskine Tate and Carroll Dickerson, and took up arranging when he moved to Washington about 1926. Did some scores for Earl Hines as a freelance, subsequently joining the band from 1932–36. Started arranging for Benny Goodman 1935, joining him full time in 1936. Left 1939 and freelanced for many leaders including Count Basie, Paul Whiteman, Gene Krupa, Bob Crosby etc. Probable that the style of some of the Swing arrangements he did for the Goodman band gave rise to the phrase 'Killer-Diller'. This could have stemmed from his *Swingtime in The Rockies* which featured Ziggy Elman at the Carnegie Hall Concert, or from *Sing Sing Sing*. Mundy did the original score for the latter, though with time it got much modified by Krupa and other soloists, till it ended more as a 'head' arrangement. During late 1950s worked in France as Musical Director for Barclay Records. Returned to New York to freelance again in the 1960s.

Oliver, Melvin James 'Sy' One of the very greatest of the arrangers of the Big Band era. He first hit fame when he joined the Jimmie Lunceford band on trumpet, and soon started contributing magnificent scores to their library—*For Dancers Only*, *My Blue Heaven*, *Four or Five Times*, *Organ Grinder's Swing*, and *By The River St. Marie* are a few. Stayed 1933–39 when he moved to Tommy Dorsey, still playing trumpet, and again boosted the band sky high with such arrangements as *Easy Does It*, *Quiet Please*, *Well Git It*, *Yes Indeed* (a score rejected by Lunceford!), and the immortal *Opus 1*. Army service 1943–45, then freelance until forming own Big Band in 1949, but seemed unable to do for himself what he had done so successfully for others. Then spent 10 years as Musical Director/Recording Supervisor for various record companies, including some studio sessions under his own name in the 1960s, while still being much in demand as an arranger. As late as 1970 had another attempt at a band of his own. Visited Britain 1974 playing trumpet in a 'Tommy Dorsey Band' led by Warren Covington, and also containing Johnny Mince (clt), Bernie Privin (tpt) and Peanuts Hucko (clt, alto).

Sy Oliver

Phillips, Sidney 'Sid' Born a Londoner (1907–75), prevented by World War I from completing his studies in Italy, so on leaving school joined small dance band on saxophone, later organizing own unit 'Sid Phillips and his Melodians' which won a *Melody Maker* contest. Took up arranging seriously in 1930, working for Lawrence Wright's publishing house till 1934, as well as for Campbell Connelly, and at the same time joined Ambrose's band (1930–39) playing baritone sax and clarinet. It was here that his composing as well as arranging talents were at their best, especially such numbers as *Cotton Picker's Congregation*, *Night Ride*, *Escapada*, *B'Wanga* and numerous others. During World War II he served in Royal Air Force, though not as a musician, but in the Intelligence Service. From 1940 onwards he started to lead small bands of his own, which from 1945 on became increasingly successful until his death in 1975. These small bands specialized in a form of 'arranged Dixieland' with Sid's clarinet always well to the fore.

Powell, Mel A fine pianist, he is included here because of his contributions to the libraries of first the Benny Goodman band (1941–43) and then the Glenn Miller band (1943–45). Perhaps his most outstanding scores were for Goodman, of his own compositions *The Earl* and *Mission to Moscow*. After the war his interests gradually took him into the realms of classical and more recently electronic music.

Redman, Donald Mathew 'Don' (alto/sop/ten/clt/tpt/voc/comp/arr) Born Piedmont, West Virginia, 1900; died 1964. Father was a music teacher, and by 12 Don was already an accomplished multi-instrumentalist. Went to New York 1923, joined Fletcher Henderson's band 1924, staying as instrumentalist, vocalist and staff arranger until 1927. Leader of McKinney's Cotton Pickers, 1927–31. Left to form own band, and took up residency at Connie's Inn, New York, 1932. Stayed, with short breaks, until disbanding in 1940. In addition to arranging for Henderson, Redman also contributed memorable scores to the libraries of Paul Whiteman, Ben Pollack, Isham Jones etc., and in the 1940s for Bobby Byrne, Jimmy Dorsey, Count Basie and Harry James. Formed band for European tour 1946–47. In 1951 became MD for singer Pearl Bailey, an association lasting many years.

Riddle, Nelson   As a trombonist, Riddle worked his way up through the Big Bands from the 1930s—he played in the trombone section of the Tommy Dorsey band that recorded Sy Oliver's *Opus One* for instance, and it was here that his arranging talents gradually became accepted. He also played for Bob Crosby, who once said '. . . we fired some pretty great arrangers too, like Ray Conniff, Henry Mancini, Nelson Riddle and Paul Weston!' In the 1940s he was playing and arranging for Charlie Spivak and later Les Elgart and Alvino Rey. His main contribution to the Big Band scene was his scoring for vocals by such as Frank Sinatra, Dinah Shore and Ella Fitzgerald. From the 1950s on he went into writing for films and TV (it was his score you heard in *Pal Joey*), and has become one of the most respected 'light' music conductors/composers/arrangers of our time.

Sampson, Edgar Melvin   After a good deal of experience as a saxophonist, came to rest for a while with the Fletcher Henderson band (1931) and started arranging. Moved to Chick Webb (1934) for whom he wrote *Stompin' At The Savoy*, *Blue Lou* and *Don't Be That Way*. In 1936 left to become a freelance arranger which he did very successfully throughout the 1940s and 1950s contributing scores to Benny Goodman, Artie Shaw, Red Norvo, Teddy Wilson and many others.

Sauter, Edward Ernest 'Eddie' Played trumpet in the 1930s and studied arranging and composition at Juillard. A spell with Charlie Barnet, but with Red Norvo as arranger from 1936–39 when he switched to Benny Goodman. During 1940s arranged for Woody Herman, Tommy Dorsey and Ray McKinley. Then in 1952 became half of the Sauter/ Finegan Orchestra (*see* Finegan) until it broke up in 1957. Spent a year as Musical Director for one of the West German radio networks, and during the 1960s mainly active in composing and scoring for films. Glenn Miller once said: 'Eddie Sauter is just about 10 years ahead of every other arranger in the business', yet probably the scores best remembered may be some of those he did for Red Norvo and Mildred Bailey—*It All Begins and Ends With You*, *A Porter's Love Song to a Chamber Maid*, *It Can Happen To You* for Mildred, and *I Would do Anything For You, Do You Ever Think of Me?* and *Remember* for the Norvo band.

Stordahl, Axel Joined Tommy Dorsey's arranging staff early on in the band's career, but finds his place here mainly as the architect of the backings for Frank Sinatra's vocals. He continued as Sinatra's Arranger/Musical Director for many years when the singer left the Dorsey band, and was responsible for most of the early hits. Like Nelson Riddle, he later became a respected conductor/composer of 'light' music.

Strayhorn, William 'Billy' A pianist, he had a good musical education, and at the age of 23 submitted his work to Duke Ellington, who was immediately impressed, and in 1939 took him on full time. He stayed with Duke until his death in 1967, and achieved the status of number two man to the master. *Lush Life*, *Chelsea Bridge*, *Johnny Come Lately*, *Day Dream* and of course, *Take The 'A' Train* live on as his memorial amongst many others.

Thornhill, Claude An excellent and much in demand session pianist in the 1930s he worked for many of the Big Bands including Ray Noble's American band. Then a spell with André Kostelanetz, which developed his arranging skills, and he was Musical Director for Maxine Sullivan. During the late 1930s he was a prolific freelance arranger for radio, films and records, mostly in Hollywood, before starting his own band in 1940, which specialized in his own scores, and featured his piano. War service in Navy, partly with Artie Shaw's Navy band. Reformed his own band in 1946, but had to disband in 1949. For part of the 1950s he was Tony Bennett's Musical Director. As an arranger he will best be remembered for *Snowfall*, his band's theme, and *A Sunday Kind of Love* with vocal by Fran Warren who sang with his post war band. Died in 1965.

Weston, Paul Finds his place because he joined Tommy Dorsey as arranger right from the beginning, and was one of those who guided the early years of the band's life. Later married Jo Stafford, Dorsey's 'Pied Piper' singer, and subsequently left to further her career as arranger/conductor, which he did very successfully throughout the 1940s and 1950s.

THE BANDS AND BANDLEADERS

Aldrich, Ronnie Now a distinguished pianist/composer/arranger/conductor in radio, TV and records, his presence in this book relates to his long association with the Squadronaires and details about him will be found under their name.

Ambrose, Albert 'Bert' (vln, 1897–1971) Born London. Emigrated to America and led a band at New York's Palais Royal 1917. Returned to England to lead band at Embassy Club in London's Bond Street 1920. Unsuccessful and returned to New York 1922, but later same year persuaded back to Embassy Club where he stayed till moving to May-

Bert Ambrose

fair Hotel 1927. Band opened with mixed US and UK musicians including Henry Levine (tpt) from US and Sidney Lipton (vln), Jack Miranda (alto, clt), Joe Crossman (ten, clt), and Dennis Radcliffe (tpt) from UK. 1928, Joe Brannelly (bjo/gtr), Perley Breed (alto), Sylvester Ahola (tpt), joined from US, with Max Bacon (drs/voc), and Ted Heath (tmb) from UK. Danny Polo (clt) from US joined 1929 as did Bert Read (pno) from UK, becoming responsible for many of the bands arrangements, and Sam Browne (voc) who stayed until 1945!

Ambrose returned to the Embassy Club 1933–36 when he went back to the Mayfair. This was probably the band's greatest period, featuring the strong trombone team of Lew Davis, Ted Heath and Tony Thorpe, Max Goldberg's trumpet, comedy from drummer Max Bacon, and the vocals of Elsie Carlisle. This was the period when Sid Phillips (bar, clt) came in and started his string of successful compositions and arrangements—*Night Ride, Cotton Picker's Congregation* etc.

A brief and unsatisfactory stay at Ciro's Club followed, then a spell at the Café de Paris (1938). Largely inactive through 1939, apart from some touring in variety and a three month stint at the Mayfair. By now Vera Lynn, Evelyn Dall and Denny Dennis were the vocal team (still with faithful Sam Browne!) From 1940 to 1945 he had to reduce to an octet. Re-started a Big Band in the 1950s but without success, and disbanded 1956 to devote his time to artist's management. Collapsed with heart attack while supervising one of his artists in a TV studio in Leeds.

Barnet, Charles Daly 'Charlie' (ten/alto/sop/voc) Born 1913. Wealthy family, money never a problem, and nicknamed 'Mad Mab', possibly to do with his

The Charlie Barnet band in the film *Idea Girl,* 1946

alleged 10 wives! Started leading a band at 16 on
cruise liners. Then played with various bands before
forming his own in 1933. This had both Eddie
Sauter and Tutti Camarata in it on trumpets, and
also arranging. Disbanded 1935 and moved to
Hollywood to try acting—*Love and Hisses* and *Sally
Irene and Mary,* both 1936 films. Back to bandleading
again, playing at Glen Island Casino, Famous
Door, Paramount Theatre New York etc. All
band's instruments and music lost in 1939 fire that
destroyed Palomar Ballroom Los Angeles where
they were playing. Both Duke Ellington and Benny
Carter helped him re-start by supplying scores for
new band. As well as this disaster, 1939 also saw the
band successful with recording of Billy May's
arrangement of *Cherokee.* Always a great Ellington
devotee, this became more and more obvious in the

band's successful follow-ups: *The Count's Idea*, *The Duke's Idea*, *Pompton Turnpike*, *Redskin Rhumba*. Their biggest hit was their 1944 recording of *Skyliner*.

Barnet continued to lead bands through the 1950s, but gradually less and less, finally retiring to Palm Springs in the 1960s. His bands have been goldmines of future talent, and he was among the first band-leaders to feature black musicians (Benny Carter, Roy Eldridge, Dizzy Gillespie, Peanuts Holland, Trummy Young etc.) and white in the same band. He also always had good singers: Mary Ann McCall, Kay Starr, Fran Warren. And many good arrangers followed Billy May including Neal Hefti and Ralph Burns.

Les Brown with the trombone section of his band

Basie, William 'Count' (pno) Born 1904. Played piano in various bands during mid 1920s before joining Bennie Moten's band in Kansas City 1929. After Moten's death in 1935 Basie took over The Barons of Rhythm at the Reno Club, Kansas City, and from then on acquired his name 'Count'. Promoted by Jazz record producer John Hammond, the Basie Band toured 1936-37 without too much success, but following personnel changes they moved into Harlem's Savoy Ballroom (see p. 173) 1938 attracting a lot of attention, and followed this with a lengthy stay at The Famous Door. With their records selling well, their future was now assured. Because of Basie's importance to the Big Band era, full details are given in the historical section (pages 86-89). Count Basie's band has appeared in a number of films, including: *Reveille With Beverly*, *Stage Door Canteen*, *Hit Parade of 1943*, *Cinderfella*, *Sex and The Single Girl*, and *One More Time*.

Brown, Les (alto) Born 1911. Organized a student band while at Duke University, The Blue Devils, and in 1936 the entire band left college as a unit to go professional. But the parents of many of the musicians decided otherwise, and after a year the band broke up. Brown did some arranging for Larry Clinton and Isham Jones, and in 1938 took over Joe Haymes' band. With help from RCA moved into the Green Room of New York's Edison Hotel. Bookings began to follow, including a stint at the 1940 New York World's Fair. That same year Doris Day, aged 17, joined the band, and it secured a coveted booking at the Glen Island Casino. By 1941 they had had hits with instrumentals like *Bizet Had His Day* and *Mexican Hat Dance*, and in 1942 appeared in the film *Seven Days Leave* with Lucille Ball. Soon Doris Day had her monster hit with

Sentimental Journey (1945), followed by the band's *I've Got My Love to Keep Me Warm*, which, though recorded in 1943, was not released until 1948! Les and the band have continued to make records and give occasional performances, but in the early 1950s he went into radio work and then TV. For many years he was Musical Director for both the Bob Hope and Dean Martin shows. Les Brown and His Band of Renown may not have been pioneers of the era as were Goodman and Dorsey, but in some ways this was the most relaxed and swinging outfit of them all, as the records still demonstrate.

Casa Loma Orchestra This band, which laid such a strong foundation for the Swing era (*see* p. 173), grew from a mid 1920s outfit called the Orange Blossoms, which contained the future Casa Lomans Pee-Wee Hunt (tmb), Pat Davis (ten), Gene Gifford (gtr/arr), and Glen Gray (ten, real name Knoblaugh), who was to become leader. In 1929 they were supposed to open a new club in Toronto called the Casa Loma. The club never did open, but the band decided to adopt the name as its own, and at the same time to become a co-operative unit, probably the first band to do so. Their peak years of success were 1930–35 (*see* pages 39–41), at which point Gene Gifford left the band. They were also the first 'Swing' band (the phrase wasn't used then) to get a radio show, *The Camel Caravan*, from which they took their theme tune, *Smoke Rings*. Although the band survived and did well financially through to the late 1940s, the big Swing bands quickly overtook them in prestige. In the middle 1950s Glen Gray returned to the recording studios to make a series of re-creations of the Big Bands, and this, with later additional sessions directed by Billy May, became the mammoth

Time–Life Swing Era series (*see* Discography). Glen Gray died 1963.

Coon-Sanders Nighthawks Formed 1918, the partners were drummer Carleton Coon (b. 1894) and pianist Joe Sanders (b. 1896). The band was at its peak during the years 1926–32. It had long residencies at The Blackhawk, Chicago, and pioneered the use of radio to exploit its music, starting on WDAF Kansas City, then WGN Chicago, finally a network show for NBC. Must have been one of the earliest bands to have a fan club (The Nighthawks Club), and set up another first with the 'radio request'. Coon died 1932, and although Sanders led bands for many years afterwards, the great days were never recaptured. He died in 1964.

Crosby, George Robert 'Bob' (voc) Born 1913, brother of the one and only Bing Crosby. Studied law, but ended up as a professional singer with

Doris Day

The Coon-Sanders Nighthawks, 1928

Anson Weeks Orchestra (1932), subsequently joining the newly formed Dorsey Brothers Orchestra. In 1935 when tenor saxist Gil Rodin was trying to keep members of Ben Pollack's Orchestra together after Pollack disbanded, they chose Bob Crosby as the 'front man' for their co-operative venture. This was a band full of talent—Eddie Miller (ten), Matty Matlock (alto, clt), Yank Lawson (tpt), Gil Bowers (pno), Nappy Lamare (gtr/voc), Dean Kincaide (arr), Ray Bauduc (drs) and Bob Haggart (bs) were among the original members. Right from the start until the draft broke up the band in 1942, both the full orchestra and the band-within-a-band, The Bobcats, were enormously successful. One has only to recall a few of their outstanding recordings: *Gin Mill Blues*, *I Hear You Talking*, *Spain*, *Mournin' Blues*, and of course the unforgettable *Big Noise from Winnetka* and *South Rampart St. Parade*. From their initial booking at the Hotel New Yorker, the band played all the best dates across the country including the Palomar Ballroom Los Angeles and the Black-hawk in Chicago. After the break-up, Bob Crosby served in the Marines. When the war was over it was never possible to rebuild this happy, zestful, swinging band of musicians. Bob himself reverted to solo singing performances and some acting, also radio and TV appearances. In London in 1957 for TV, and also occasionally re-formed a band for Jazz festivals and special occasions. Some of the musicians are still playing, some retired. Among the former are two notables—Yank Lawson and Bob Haggart, both playing in the 1970s with the so-called World's Greatest Jazzband.

Dorsey, James 'Jimmy' (alto/clt) Born 1904. Elder brother of Tommy Dorsey. Formed Dorsey's Novelty Six *c.* 1917, and later Dorsey's Wild

Bob Crosby and the Bobcats in the film *When You're Smiling*, 1950

Canaries. From then until the formation of The Dorsey Brothers Orchestra in 1934, Jimmy Dorsey worked with various bands such as Jean Goldkette, Paul Whiteman, Red Nichols, Ted Lewis etc., and his output as a Jazz musician and session recording man was prolific. The two brothers had often formed The Dorsey Brothers Orchestra for records and other work starting in the late 1920s, but it went full time in 1934. It was unusual in that it only had one trumpet (George Thow), though the then standard 3 trombones, 4 saxes and 4 rhythm were present, Glenn Miller being in the trombone section, and being responsible for many of the band's arrangements. Among the best were *Stop, Look, and Listen*, *By Heck*, *Dippermouth Blues* and *Eccentric*. On some records the band was augmented by additional brass. Amongst their most attractive performances were some of those done in an accompanying capacity to The Boswell Sisters. It is said that the routines for many of these were done by Connie and her piano playing sister Martha, in collaboration with Tommy and Glenn Miller.

The crunch came for Jimmy one night in the summer of 1935, when Tommy stormed off the stand during their engagement at Glen Island Casino, and subsequently formed a band of his own. Jimmy, a reluctant bandleader by all accounts, picked up the pieces, brought in Bobby Byrne to play trombone and saw out the summer season at Glen Island. For the next 18 months they were based in Los Angeles, having captured the Bing Crosby *Kraft Music Hall* radio series. Jimmy built up a good band, which included Ray McKinley on drums, the singing of Bob Eberly and later Helen O'Connell, and Toots Camarata on first trumpet and in charge of arranging. The usual round of one-night stands and residencies began, and there were successful records, notably the duets by Bob and Helen—*Green Eyes*, *Amapola*, *Tangerine* etc.

As a band, it never seemed during this period (1937–42) to be able to make up its mind as to its style, playing a mixture of 2–beat Dixie and 4–beat Swing intrumentals, and resting for much of its success on the popularity of its singing team, both on record and personally. In 1943 Eberly was drafted and Helen O'Connell left to be replaced by Kitty Kallen. The band at last developed a style, and there were personnel changes. Babe Russin (ten), Nat Kazebier (tpt), Johnny Guanieri (pno), Herb Ellis (gtr) were among those responsible, and through to 1946 Jimmy rivalled Tommy in the popularity polls. From then on however the band, like so many others, seemed to decline, and apart from his record of *So Rare* (1956) the magic was gone. From 1953–56 Jimmy and Tommy were reunited in a new Dorsey Brothers Orchestra, but for both of them the Big Band era was over, and Jimmy died after a lengthy illness in 1957, outliving Tommy by only six months. The Jimmy Dorsey Band appeared in several films, including *Shall We Dance*, *The Fleet's In*, *Four Jacks and a Jeep*, and Jimmy of course in *The Fabulous Dorseys*.

Dorsey, Thomas 'Tommy' (tmb) Born 1905. Younger brother of Jimmy Dorsey. For details of The Dorsey Brothers Orchestra *see* under Jimmy Dorsey. The Tommy Dorsey Orchestra has also been examined in some detail in our historical section (*see* pages 65–69). The first Tommy Dorsey band, which opened at the Blue Room of the Hotel Lincoln in New York in 1936, did not set the world alight, though from the beginning he had Paul

Tommy and Jimmy Dorsey in the film *The Fabulous Dorseys*, 1946

Weston on his arranging staff and Edythe Wright as vocalist. However they achieved success with their third recording session, which produced their theme, *I'm Getting Sentimental Over You*. Personnel changes, especially those that brought in Bunny Berigan (tpt), Bud Freeman (ten) and Dave Tough (drs), with Jack Leonard (voc) soon paid off, and 1937 saw their big hit record of *Marie*. In 1939 both Edythe Wright and Jack Leonard left, the latter being replaced by Frank Sinatra (Axel Stordahl who did Frank's early arrangements was already with the band) in 1940, and Edythe by Jo Stafford leading the vocal group, The Pied Pipers. A band-within-a-band, The Clambake Seven, was already featured in Jazz numbers—good proof that Tommy played excellent Jazz trombone when required.

Probably the Dorsey band was at its height during the years 1940–46 (apart from a dip in success 1942–43 when Sinatra left and several good musicians were drafted). Sy Oliver joined the arranging staff, and this was the period that produced *I'll Never Smile Again* (Frank Sinatra), *Yes Indeed* (band), *For You* (Jo Stafford), *There Are Such Things* (Sinatra with The Pied Pipers) and of course the immortal *Opus 1* (band), and *On The Sunny Side of The Street* (The Sentimentalists, who had replaced The Pied Pipers). Both the latter could be described as 'Sy Oliver's greatest hits'. Tommy had always interested himself in the business aspects of his band. Early on he signed with MCA, one of the two biggest band agencies in the US (Jimmy was with the other, GAC), and appeared to hate them from that day forth. When the contract finally expired he took a trade paper advertisement that said 'Whew . . . I'm finally out of the clutches of you know who!' Similarly in 1944 after a row with the Hollywood Palladium where he was playing, he went out and bought his own ballroom—The Casino Gardens, nearby in Ocean Park.

But at the end of 1946 like so many others, Tommy Dorsey disbanded. He attempted several new bands, but without any great success, and between 1953 and 1956 was reunited with his brother (*see* under Jimmy Dorsey). The band appeared in the films *Las Vegas Nights*, *Girl Crazy*, *Dubarry Was a Lady*, *Broadway Rhythm* and *A Song is Born*. Tommy of course was also in *The Fabulous Dorseys*. He died in November 1956, choking to death in his sleep. Shortly afterwards a star studded group of musicians and singers staged a Tommy Dorsey Memorial Concert. Jackie Gleason introduced it, and in his closing lines said: 'I wish I could say, the way the announcers used to do, "Join us again tomorrow night for more music by Tommy Dorsey and His Orchestra." But I can't, because there are no tomorrows left for us with Tommy . . . Goodnight everybody.'

Ellington, Edward Kennedy 'Duke' (pno/arr/comp, 1899–1971) Born Washington, D.C. Duke Ellington and His Orchestra have been extensively covered in our historical section (pages 29–34), so to avoid duplication only highlights of his career are given here. 1923 at The Hollywood Club, New York, with The Washingtonians. 1925–27 touring and residencies mainly in Massachusetts, New England and New York, including the Kentucky Club (the Hollywood renamed) and other clubs, ballrooms and theatres. 1927–31 resident at The Cotton Club, but time off for tours (California) film work etc. 1933 British tour including London Palladium, and a concert in Paris. Touring and residencies throughout the US and Canada 1933–39. 1939 toured France, Belgium, Holland, Denmark

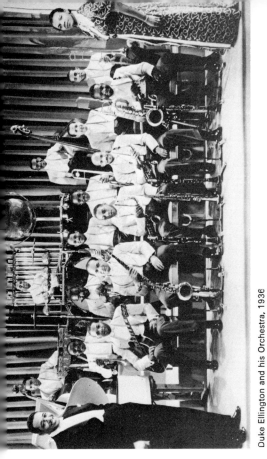

Duke Ellington and his Orchestra, 1936

and Sweden. 1941 appeared in *Jump for Joy* in Los Angeles. 1943, Carnegie Hall Concert. More touring and residencies throughout the US up to 1947. British tour 1948. Throughout 1950s and 1960s concentrated more and more on composing and making concert appearances throughout the world including Britain (1958, several in the 1960s), the rest of Europe, the Far East, Middle East, India, Japan, South America and in 1970 Australia and New Zealand.

Among his many compositions the following are well known: *Mood Indigo, Solitude, Sophisticated Lady, I Got it Bad and That ain't Good, It Don't Mean a Thing, Do Nothing Till You Hear From Me, Don't Get Around Much Any More,* and *Caravan.* Extended works include: *Black Brown and Beige, The Tattooed Bride, Such Sweet Thunder, Harlem, Suite Thursday, Impressions of The Far East, New Orleans Suite,* and *In The Beginning God.* He wrote film music for *Anatomy of a Murder, Paris Blues,* and several stage productions including *Jump for Joy* and *Beggar's Holiday.* His film appearances include: *Check and Double Check, Murder At The Vanities, Belle of the 90s, Cabin in The Sky, Reveille with Beverly,* as well as *Anatomy of a Murder* and *Paris Blues.* He has been commemorated on postage stamps, and at least 5 books have been written about him (*see* Bibliography). Little enough in return for what he gave to those who loved his music and his Orchestra.

Europe, James Reese (pno/vln, 1881–1919)   Born Alabama, moved early to Washington where he received musical training, and went to New York in 1904. He is included here as being a pioneer of Big Bands, albeit not as we now know them. Formed a band in 1910, and in 1914 appointed Musical Director to the dance team of Vernon and Irene

Castle. In same year presented a concert at Carnegie Hall. It may or may not have been Jazz, but it contained 10 pianos, 7 cornets, 8 trombones, and heaps of banjos, mandolins, etc. When the US entered the First World War he was appointed a Lieutenant and directed the 369th Infantry Regiment Band, touring Europe. The band returned to the US 1919 and during a triumphant tour of American cities he was stabbed in his dressing room by one of the drummers in the band, dying shortly afterwards. Recorded for Victor (US) 1915–16, and for Pathé (US) 1919. Certainly a pioneer.

Fox, Roy (cor/tpt)   Born 1901, Denver, Colorado. Family moved to Hollywood and he took up cornet at 11, playing professionally with Abe Lyman at 17. 1920, led own band in Culver City, Los Angeles, Miami and New York. Short period as a Musical Director at Fox Films (no relation). While there offered 8 week engagement at Café de Paris, London. Arrived with 8-piece American Band 1930, billed as 'The Whispering Cornetist', and using *Whispering* as his signature tune. Engagement not satisfactory, but stayed on as Decca offered him a recording contract 1931 using British musicians, and same year took band into the Monseigneur Restaurant for its opening. Period 1931–34 covered in historical section (pages 52–53). 1934–38 band toured UK consistently, then Fox left for Australia. During the Second World War led small groups in New York, returning to UK 1946, but attempts to form bands in London not successful. He gradually phased himself out of music and into artist's management during the 1950s and 1960s. Now retired but still lives in England. Among representative recordings are *Whispering* (1931, on which his speaking voice is heard as well as his cornet), *Georgia* and

143

How'm I Doin' (1932, both featuring Nat Gonella), *You're My Everything* (voc: Al Bowlly), and *June in January* (1933, voc: Denny Dennis).

Geraldo, real name Gerald Bright, (pno, 1904–1975) Born London. Studied at Royal Academy of Music, and had first professional jobs playing piano and organ in silent cinemas and restaurants. Formed various dance band combinations during the 1920s, but decided to go Latin-American and in 1930 took his Gaucho Tango Band into the Savoy Hotel opposite the Savoy Orpheans. By 1937 he had changed policy to a standard dance band. Details of the period 1939–55 are given in our historical section (page 97), and from then onwards Geraldo concentrated mainly on his booking agency, and on giving occasional concert performances. He was always a prolific broadcaster, and in particular he will be remembered with affection for the years 1942–48 when he was often on the air three times per week with shows ranging from straight band broadcasts to *Dancing Through* (60 minutes of non-stop music) with an enlarged band and *Tip Top Tunes* which used a concert-sized orchestra. Among his singers Len Camber, Dorothy Carless, and her sister Carole Carr were outstanding, as was the voice of David Miller who produced and introduced the broadcasts, Gerry himself rarely speaking on the air until the 1950s.

Goldkette, Jean (pno, 1899–1962) Born in France and lived in Greece and Russia before moving to America 1911. Began playing professionally in Chicago, then moved to Detroit 1921 where he owned the Greystone Ballroom. As well as running a band of his own he began controlling numerous others including McKinney's Cotton

Pickers, and The Orange Blossoms, which later became the Casa Loma Orchestra. 1926 decided to have a Big Band full of Jazz stars and try to outdo Paul Whiteman. Among the musicians were Bix Beiderbecke (cor), Jimmy and Tommy Dorsey (alto/clt and tmb), Joe Venuti (vln), Eddie Lang (gtr), Frankie Trumbauer (C Mel sax/alto), Pee-Wee Russell (ten/clt), Russ Morgan (tmb), and Don Murray (alto/clt), and most of the original Wolverines Orchestra. After this magnificent venture collapsed financially (*see* historical section, pages 22–23), Goldkette remained active in music for some time, mainly as a band booker, but concentrating on playing solo piano himself in classical works (he appeared with the Detroit Symphony Orchestra in 1930).

Goodman, Benjamin David 'Benny' (clt/alto) Born Chicago, 1909. Early career as a Jazz musician. Started his first Big Band Oct 1934 for Billy Rose's Music Hall, New York. Band regularly featured on NBC's *Let's Dance* coast-to-coast radio show, from which he subsequently took his theme tune. First nationwide tour began May 1935. Not very successful—in Denver patrons asked for their money back! On 21st August he opened at the Palomar Ballroom, Los Angeles. Personnel: Nate Kazebier, Bunny Berigan, Ralph Muzillo (tpts); Red Ballard, Jack Lacey (tmbs); Hymie Schertzer, Bill de Pew (altos); Arthur Rollini, Dick Clark (tens); Jess Stacy (pno); Alan Reuss (gtr); Harry Goodman (Benny's brother, bs); Gene Krupa (drs). The evening started with an unenthusiastic audience. Benny, thinking this was going to be another 'duff' date, of which they'd had so many, threw caution to the winds and put on his Fletcher Henderson arrangement of *King Porter Stomp*. The Ballroom erupted. The cheers and

The Benny Goodman Trio in the film *The Benny Goodman Story*

screams from around the bandstand were picked up and broadcast by NBC's mics, and this enthusiasm, heard nationwide, brought out the customers in thousands for the remaining tour dates. A three week booking at Chicago's Congress Hotel lasted eight months! Swing had suddenly been born, and Benny Goodman was the King.

1936, first film, *The Big Broadcast of 1937*, followed by many more including *The Benny Goodman Story*, 1955. Also 1936, the first Quartet records: Goodman (clt), Teddy Wilson (pno), Lionel Hampton (vibes), Gene Krupa (drs)—the Trio records were 1935. 1938 saw the famous Carnegie Hall concert. Writing of the event the magazine *Metronome* said that the Goodman band would be 'replacing Jack Barbirolli and his Philharmonic Cats, the regular band in that spot'. In addition to the Goodman band guest musicians included: Johnny Hodges (alto), Harry Carney (bar) and 'Cootie' Williams (tpt), all from the Duke Ellington band; Count Basie on piano with Lester Young (ten), Buck Clayton (tpt) and his rhythm section: Freddie Green (gtr), Walter Page (bs); also Bobby Hackett (cor). The number that climaxed the show, *Sing Sing Sing* was a performance unequalled in the annals of Swing. During their engagement at New York's Paramount Theatre police had to be called to control the crowds of bobbysoxers who, having queued outside from 7 am to get in, started jitterbugging in the aisles when they were in. Who said Frank Sinatra started mass hysteria?

CARNEGIE HALL PROGRAM
SEASON 1937-1938

FIRE NOTICE—Look around *now* and choose the nearest exit to your seat. In case of fire walk (not run) to *that* Exit. Do not try to beat your neighbor to the street.

JOHN J. McELLIGOTT, *Fire Commissioner*

CARNEGIE HALL

Sunday Evening, January 16th, at 8:30

S. HUROK

presents

(by arrangement with Music Corporation of America)

BENNY GOODMAN
and his
SWING ORCHESTRA

I.

"Don't Be That Way" .... *Edgar Sampson*
"Sometimes I'm Happy" (from "Hit the Deck") ...... *Irving Caesar &*
Vincent Youmans
"One O'clock Jump" .... *William (Count) Basie*

II.

TWENTY YEARS OF JAZZ

"Sensation Rag" (as played c. 1917 by the Dixieland Jazz Band)
E. B. Edwards

PROGRAM CONTINUED ON SECOND PAGE FOLLOWING

Programme for Benny Goodman's concert at the Carnegie Hall, January 1938

During the next two years many departures from the band forced a break-up. The same year Goodman appeared as clarinet soloist with New York Philharmonic Orchestra at Carnegie Hall in Mozart's Clarinet Concerto. 1941 formed new band with Eddie Sauter as arranger. Personnel: Billy Butterfield, Jimmy Maxwell, 'Cootie' Williams (tpts); Lou McGarity, Cutty Cutshall (tmbs); Les Robinson, Gene Kinsey (altos); Georgie Auld, Pete Mondello (tens); Skip Martin (bar); Mel Powell (pno); Charlie Christian (gtr); Artie Bernstein (bs); Sid Catlett (drs); Peggy Lee (voc). This band and Benny's 'Palomar' band are generally rated as his two best by critics.

1942 married Alice Duckworth, John Hammond's sister (Jazz producer Hammond had done much for Benny's career as he had for many other artists). Continued leading bands for next eight years, then a period of selected tours: London Palladium (soloist only) 1949; Europe 1950; Japan, Far East 1956–57; Europe 1958–59; USSR 1962; Japan 1964; Belgium 1966; Europe 1970; last London concert, Oct. 1974, Royal Albert Hall. Space does not permit a listing of the star musicians who have passed through Benny Goodman's Bands through the years, but one must mention some super stars: Bunny Berigan, Harry James, Ziggy Elman and 'Cootie' Williams among the trumpets; Jess Stacy, Teddy Wilson (pno); Gene Krupa (dms); Lionel Hampton (vibes); Charlie Christian (gtr), and of course Peggy Lee among the singers.

Benny Goodman continues to do occasional concert performances, but is now semi-retired. Film appearances include: *Hollywood Hotel*, *Stage Door Canteen*, *Sweet and Lowdown*, and a solo appearance in *A Song is Born*, plus those mentioned earlier. For books on Benny Goodman *see* Bibliography.

Hampton, Lionel (vibes/drs) Born 1909, Louisville, Kentucky. Educated in Chicago and Wisconsin where he learned to play drums and xylophone. Various jobs with bands around Chicago then moved to California 1927. From 1929 long spell in band at Sebastian's Cotton Club, Culver City, especially under Les Hite, and recorded with Louis Armstrong (1930). Formed bands for various jobs until joining Benny Goodman in 1936, staying till 1940 when he left for Los Angeles to form his own band. The band started off well driven by Hamp's extrovert personality, and a hit record *Flyin' Home* in 1942 set the seal on their success. Lionel Hampton has continued to lead swinging and often exciting bands through the 1950s and 1960s. Further details in our historical section (page 86).

Lionel Hampton

Heath, Edward 'Ted' (tmb, 1900–69) Born London. His father was leader of the Wandsworth Borough Band, and at 10 Ted won a prize for playing tenor horn in a brass band contest. Switched to trombone in early teens, and frequently had to play as a street musician due to lack of work. Claimed to have heard the Original Dixieland Jazz Band by playing outside Hammersmith Palais in 1919! While playing as street musician, discovered by Jack Hylton, with whom he played from 1922. Spell with Bert Firman 1924–25, then back to Hylton till 1927 when he joined Ambrose where he stayed till 1935. Then worked with various bands including Sydney Lipton and Geraldo.

Encouraged by the BBC and Decca Records, he formed a broadcasting and recording band in 1944, the initial titles *Opus 1* and *My Guy's Come Back* achieving considerable praise, and the band began to be compared with Charlie Barnet and Woody

Ted Heath,
1956

Herman. But it was a hard struggle and work did not come along. With his wife Moira Ted wrote a hit song *That Lovely Weekend* (originally banned by the BBC!), and decided to use the royalties from that to have a last attempt at financing the band on a permanent basis. Aided by more dates on radio and more records, engagements began to come in, and soon the band was acclaimed as the best outside the US.

Over the years a long catalogue of fine soloists have played in Ted Heath's bands—Kenny Baker, Ronnie Scott, Tommy Whittle, Jack Parnell, Eddie Blair, Henry McKenzie are just a few, and the 1950s singing team of Lita Roza, Dickie Valentine and Dennis Lotis had many hit records of their own, in addition to numerous instrumentals by the band. The long running series of London Palladium Swing Sessions, accompanying performers like Ella Fitzgerald, and contributions to the library from Americans like Tadd Dameron as well as Britain's Johnny Dankworth, Kenny Graham, Johnny Keating, Reg Owen and Ralph Dollimore all built up the prestige of the band.

In 1956 Ted was the first to break through the MU/AF of M ban, and took the band to the US in exchange for Stan Kenton's band, which visited England. This was only the first of many such international tours. Throughout the 1950s and early 1960s Ted's band was rated among the top four in the world, and only ill health forced him to give it up. He died at Virginia Water, Surrey, on 18th November 1969.

Henderson, James Fletcher 'Smack' (pno/comp/ arr, 1898–1952) Born Cuthbert, Georgia and educated locally, moving to Atlanta Morehouse College 1916. In New York 1920. Worked for a music publisher, then for Black Swan Record Company, forming own band 1921 (The Black Swan Troubadours) to accompany Ethel Waters. Took resident band into Roseland Ballroom 1924 and with time off for occasional tours and other New York dates, remained there until 1934. He began arranging in the early 1930s, and apart from his now well known work for Benny Goodman he also supplied arrangements for Teddy Hill, Will Bradley, Isham Jones, The Casa Loma Orchestra and Jack Hylton. In spite of having supplied arrangements for Goodman from 1935, he was on Benny's full-time staff only from 1939–41. Led bands of his own through the 1940s with one further spell of a year on the Goodman staff, and toured again with Ethel Waters 1948–49. Suffered a stroke 1950 resulting in partial paralysis and was unable to work again. Fletcher Henderson's importance to the Big Band era can hardly be overestimated, in spite of what appears to be modest achievements as set out here. His early scores for Benny Goodman undoubtedly sparked off the whole thing, and his band was always a nursery for brilliant Jazz musicians. For further details *see* historical section (pages 26–28).

Herman, Charles Woodrow 'Woody' (clt/voc) Born 1913. Worked in variety as a child prodigy, taking up saxophone and clarinet and incorporating them into his singing act. Began playing professionally *c* 1928 with various bands including a spell with Gus Arnheim, and then Isham Jones (1934–36). When Jones disbanded Woody and five other members of the band got together to form a co-operative unit, playing with some success, and it was an enlarged version of this group that became 'The Band That Plays The Blues' in 1937. From then onwards Woody's career is examined in our historical section (pages 76–79). Space precludes us from repeating this information, but it is interesting to note: 1940, band chosen by Igor Stravinsky to play first performance of his *Ebony Concerto* at Carnegie Hall. During the years 1939–45 the band played every major venue including The Roseland Ballroom, Frank Dailey's Meadowbrook, Glen Island Casino, Chicago's Sherman Hotel, and The Famous Door. Once asked why he gave up playing sax and concentrated on clarinet Woody replied: 'I sounded like Bud Freeman with his hands chopped off!'

Hylton, Jack (pno, 1892–1965) Born near Bolton, Lancashire. His early life and career up to 1939 are covered in our historical section (pages 45–47). The last performance of the great Hylton band was a

Fletcher
Henderson

Jack Hylton,
1924

concert at the Paris Opera House as late as April 1940. Then the band broke up and Jack developed the interest he had always had in stage shows, becoming a very successful impresario during the 1950s and 1960s. This culminated in his production of *Camelot* at the Theatre Royal Drury Lane in 1964. Earlier highlights associated with this remarkable man included leading one of the first British bands to record (1921), and under the title Hylton's Rhythmagicians a classic British Jazz record of *Grievin' For You*, featuring Jack Jackson (tpt), E. O. Pogson (alto/clt), Lew Davis (tmb) and Hugo Rignold (vln). It has been said that in the year 1929 the band gave 700 performances, travelled 63,000 miles and sold a total of 3,180,000 records! 1930, decorated for his services to France and to music. 1931, first British band to broadcast direct to the US. 1939 appeared in the film *Bandwagon*. 1950 conducted for a Royal Command Performance at the London

Palladium. Remembered by most who played for him as a tough, but very sympathetic boss.

Jackson, Jack (tpt/arr/voc, 1906–78)   Born Barnsley, Yorkshire. Early in life played in brass bands, then studied trumpet at Royal Academy of Music. Early professional jobs on cruise liners, then with a variety of bands including Bert Ralton's Savoy Havana Band, Jack Hylton (1927), Jack Payne (1931–33) as well as appearing prolifically in the recording studios with other bands, notably Fred Elizalde and Ambrose. Formed own band 1933 for the Dorchester Hotel where he stayed till 1939. A year's touring followed, then a residency at the Mayfair Hotel from 1940. During latter war years did cartoon work for Ministry of Information, being a talented artist as well as a musician. Briefly led a small band at Churchill's Club 1947, before disbanding to become England's number one disc jockey from 1948 through the 1950s and 1960s. Retired to Canary Islands, but suffered ill health and returned to England where he continued to give occasional radio programmes until his death.

James, Harry Hagg (tpt)   Born Albany, Georgia 1916. Came from a circus family, where father conducted the band. Took trumpet lessons from dad and began playing professionally 1931. Joined Ben Pollack's band 1935, where he was heard by Benny Goodman whom he joined in 1936, remaining till 1939. Same year opened with his own band at the Benjamin Franklin Hotel, Philadelphia. With his own outfit he deliberately changed his trumpet style. With Goodman he had been featured in many Jazz choruses. While still playing as forcibly as ever when occasion demanded, he began featuring himself more in slow ballads, something which he developed further by blending his trumpet with his singers, Dick Haymes and Helen Forrest, the team which replaced Frank Sinatra.

Sinatra was heard by James singing on the *Dance Parade* programme on New York's station WNEW, and joined the band in June 1939. However the James band was only starting, and when the offer from the well established Tommy Dorsey came for Frank to join him in 1940, Harry gave Frank his blessing, knowing what it would mean to be the main singer with the Dorsey band. It took a little while after Sinatra's departure to establish the trumpet plus vocal idea, but with the success of the James/Forrest record of *I Don't Want to Walk Without You* in 1942, the seal was set. Later that same year the band unseated Glenn Miller as the winner of the *Make Believe Ballroom* favourite band poll. And to follow success with success, their record

Harry James

Dick Haymes
and Helen
Forrest

of *I've Heard that Song Before* sold 1,250,000 copies,
they took over the Chesterfield cigarettes radio show
from Glenn Miller when he went into the Army,
and grabbed the Coca Cola show as well!

But 1943 saw the draft take some of Harry's best
musicians, and with the AF of M ban on recording
in operation 1944 saw the band in decline, though
still getting plenty of work. By 1945 there were signs
that James was losing interest in the band business,
and the break-up came in 1946.

However, in 1947 he had a band again, and
continued on and off through the 1950s, but the
great days were gone beyond recall. From 1957 when
the band made a European tour, he has concentrated
on special occasions, plus lengthy seasons in Nevada

through the 1960s. Married Betty Grable 1943. Later divorced. Appeared in several films including *Springtime in the Rockies* and *The Benny Goodman Story*. In case anyone thinks that Harry James could not play brilliant Jazz, they should listen to some of his solo work with Benny Goodman, and to his own record of *Feet Draggin' Blues*.

Jones, Isham (ten/arr/comp, 1893–1956) Born Coalton, Iowa. Began leading his own bands around Chicago during First World War, and was one of the first leaders to write his own arrangements, and it is because of his insistence throughout his career on the importance of scoring for a dance band that he merits his place here. He consistently had the best arrangers of his time working for him, including in later years such well known names as Joe Bishop, Victor Young and Gordon Jenkins.

Musically the band, excellent though it was,

Isham Jones

does not fall within the scope of this book, though in addition to its emphasis on good arrangements, it must be noted that during its peak years of 1926–36 it contained such later to be discovered stars as Jack Jenney (tmb, Shaw, Goodman), Pee-Wee Erwin (tpt, Goodman, Dorsey), George Thow (tpt, Dorsey Bros.) and Woody Herman. Herman's first band was made round a nucleus of ex-Isham Jones men: Joe Bishop (arr/tuba/flugelhorn), Saxey Mansfield (ten), Clarence Willard and Kermit Simmons (tpts), Neal Reid (tmb), Nick Hupfer (vln), Walter Yoder (bs), and Frankie Carlson (drs). Jones was also a well known composer, and *I'll See You in My Dreams*, *It Had to Be You*, *The One I Love Belongs to Somebody Else*, *On the Alamo*, *Swingin' Down The Lane*, *You've Got Me Cryin' Again* etc, will be well remembered. Curiously, the band also made the first hit record of Hoagy Carmichael's song *Stardust*.

Kenton, Stanley 'Stan the Man' (pno/arr/comp) Born 1912. Played piano in various bands in the 1930s including Gus Arnheim for whom he did arrangements. Started his own band 1940, and took first resident season 1941 at the Rendezvous Ballroom, Balboa. Broadcasts on Station KHJ and a recording contract with Capitol began to get the band talked about. Stan Kenton himself has described his band as being on a 'progressive' path right from its beginning, and as such it only fits marginally into this book. The band and its musical policy are discussed in our historical section (page 104).

Krupa, Eugene 'Gene' (drs, 1909–1973) Born Chicago. Started drumming during schooldays, studying percussion 1925, but still keeping up band work. Played with various bands around Chicago, moving to New York 1929. Started playing with Red Nichols, which let him in on studio session work. Played with various commercial dance bands until joining Benny Goodman in 1934. Left 1938 to form own band, opening at the Steel Pier in Atlantic City. The band got off to a fine start and other good dates quickly followed. Gene built up a band of good musicians, and aided by two strong personalities in Anita O'Day (voc) and Roy Eldridge (tpt/voc) enjoyed considerable success till 1943 when he was jailed on a charge of possessing marijuana. In 1944 he started again, building up yet another good band, this time more jazz orientated, and gradually taking into account some of the younger generation of Bop musicians (including Gerry Mulligan) and some more traditionally minded youngsters like Charlie Ventura (ten) and Buddy de Franco (clt). The band finally folded in 1951, Gene then concentrating on working with a trio, and being frequently featured in Norman Granz's *Jazz at The Philharmonic* package. He suffered a stroke in 1960 which caused him to reduce his work load, but his health gradually deteriorated and he died in 1973. He made some film appearances, including *George White's Scandals*, *Some Like it Hot*, *The Benny Goodman Story*, and *The Gene Krupa Story*—retitled *Drum Crazy* in some countries.

Lunceford, James Melvin 'Jimmie' (alto/arr, 1902–1947) Born Fulton, Missouri, educated in Denver, Colorado, but took a degree in music at Fisk University (1926). Formed first band of students while teaching in Memphis. After going professional, touring and residencies followed until the band got its big break in 1934 when it took over from Duke Ellington at The Cotton Club.

The Lunceford band was never a collection of

Jazz stars like some others, but always concentrated on a highly polished and efficient but very swinging ensemble sound. Its first two records *White Heat* and *Jazznochracy* arranged by Will Hudson demonstrate its efficiency, but not the Swing that was to follow when Sy Oliver joined on trumpet and started writing for the outfit (1934). The peak years of the Lunceford band were undoubtedly between then and Oliver leaving to join Tommy Dorsey in 1939. From then on, although successful financially, the band was on a slow musical decline until Jimmie's death from a heart attack in 1947.

Undoubtedly one of the things that gradually wore the band down was its punishing schedule of one-night stands. Most of the big white bands could count on seasons of sometimes many weeks in one venue. But the black bands were *persona non grata* in such establishments and had to rely on one-nighters for their living, and the more popular the band, the greater the amount of travelling involved. Next only to Ellington and Basie, the Jimmie Lunceford Band was the greatest black band of them all.

Jimmie
Lunceford

Miller, Alton Glenn (tmb/arr/comp, 1904–1944) Born Clarinda, Iowa. Began playing cornet and mandolin, but switched to trombone 1916. First professional job 1921. Played with various bands until joining Ben Pollack 1926, leaving the band 1928 in New York. Found his way into the radio and recording scene, including work with Red Nichols. Worked in theatre pit bands through early 1930s and did a lot of freelance arranging before joining the Dorsey Brothers Orchestra 1934. Left Dorseys 1935 to organize band for Ray Noble at the Rainbow Room, playing in trombone section himself, and contributing many arrangements. Left Noble 1937 to start own band. Glenn Miller is so important to the Big Band scene that the rest of his career is dealt with as fully as space permits in our historical section—*see* pages 92–95.

Noble, Ray (pno/arr/comp, 1907–78) Born Brighton, Sussex. Studied piano and became interested in dance music, winning *Melody Maker* arranging competition 1927. Then worked for a music publisher, and contributed arrangements for many bands especially Jack Payne. 1929 appointed Musical Director of His Master's Voice Records (now EMI). In this capacity commenced a series of very popular recordings with a studio band of session musicians, mainly of his own compositions but also playing his arrangements of the best of the hits of the day.

Finding his records selling phenomenally well in the US as well as in the UK, he went to New York in 1934, taking with him singer Al Bowlly, and drummer Bill Harty, and led a star studded band assembled for him by Glenn Miller, who played in the trombone section and contributed many arrangements. The band opened at the Rainbow

Room, New York's plushest location on top of the RCA/Radio City building. In spite of the presence in the band of Will Bradley (tmb), Charlie Spivak (tpt), Bud Freeman (ten), Johnny Mince (clt) and Claude Thornhill (pno/arr), it was a Sweet styled band, and as such only marginally within the scope of this book.

When the band broke up *c* 1936, Noble went to live in California, working as a Musical Director in radio, and continuing to compose. In the 1960s he retired to live in Jersey in the Channel Islands, but *c* 1970 returned to the US to live in Santa Barbara. Among his best known compositions are: *Goodnight Sweetheart*, *Love is The Sweetest Thing*, *By The Fireside*, *The Very Thought of You*, *The Touch of Your Lips*, and *Cherokee*.

Shaw, Arthur Jacob 'Artie' (real name Arshawsky, clt/alto/comp) Born 1910, New York. Started playing saxophone aged 12, joining school band and winning talent contest. Left home 1925 and played with various bands including Paul Specht and Roger Wolfe Kahn to 1931 when he joined Red Nichols. Briefly with Roger Wolfe Kahn again 1933, then freelance radio and recording work to 1936 when he started his first band. From then on his story is dealt with in our historical section (*see* pages 71–2). After 1953 he left music and turned to dairy farming, moving to Spain in 1955 and back to the US 1960. Married to actress Evelyn Keyes, lives in Connecticut and writes. Previously a much married man, including Lana Turner and Ava Gardner. Published his autobiography *The Trouble with Cinderella* in 1952.

Skyrockets Formed 1940 in Blackpool by a number of musicians who found themselves together undergoing training to work on balloons, thus giving themselves an off-duty musical outlet. Real title was The Number 1 Balloon Centre Dance Orchestra, and the musicians who formed it ultimately found themselves based at Kidbrooke, near London. The Air Ministry heard of the venture and arranged for the band to undertake a series of propaganda broadcasts to the Germans. Further broadcasting and recording followed, and 1942 band booked to appear at the Jazz Jamboree. Apart from its very early days the band's leader was Paul Fenhoulet (tmb/arr), who had spent many pre-war years with the bands of Jack Hylton and Carroll Gibbons. Other well known names in the band included Les Lambert (tpt), Don McCaffer (tmb), Pat Dodd (pno), and Pat Smuts (ten). On demobilization 13 of the musicians decided to form themselves into a co-operative unit. 1946 saw them established in the pit of the London Palladium. Paul Fenhoulet left in 1947, to be replaced by Woolf Phillips (tmb, brother of Sid). The band broke up in the 1950s.

Squadronaires Formed in 1939 at the suggestion of Sir Walford Davies, Master of the King's Musick. For details *see* our historical section, pages 91–93. Lack of space prevents us from repeating the story here, but we should take a look at the personnel and the music they made. This was undoubtedly Britain's all-star band. By 1942 when their now famous recording of *South Rampart St. Parade* was made, the musicians were: Archie Craig, Tommy McQuater (tpts); George Chisholm, Eric Breeze (tmbs); Tommy Bradbury, Harry Lewis (altos); Jimmy Durant (ten/sop); Andy McDevitt (ten/clt); Ronnie Aldrich (pno); Sid Colin (gtr); Arthur Maden (bs); Jock Cummings (drs). By 1947, two years after demobilization, all the above were still there except Harry Lewis (invalided out) and Sid Colin (left to become a writer), and in 1944 in had come: Clinton Ffrench and Jimmy Watson to make 4 trumpets; and Monty Levy (alto) and Cliff Townshend (bar/alto/clt) to make 5 saxes. Not long after demobilization Jimmy Miller, their original leader, left, and Ronnie Aldrich, who with George Chisholm had been responsible for most of the band's scores, took over and guided their destiny until they finally broke up in 1964. Ronnie was born at Erith, Kent in 1916. He was taught piano and violin as a boy, but took up saxes, playing in India. Returned to the UK, switched back to piano as accompanist to Elsie Carlisle and Sam Browne. Then theatre and film work until 1939. The Squadronaires' greatest days lasted from 1941 to the mid 1950s, and a study of the Discography will be well repaid, because this band, after Lew Stone and Ambrose in the mid 1930s, was almost certainly Britain's finest Big Band until the peak of the Ted Heath orchestra in the mid 1950s.

Stone, Lew (pno/arr, 1898–1969) Born London. First professional job with Bert Ralton's Savoy Havana Band on piano. He also started to do arrangements. By 1927 he was writing for many bands, some of his best work being for Ambrose. 1931 temporarily gave up arranging to join Roy Fox as pianist. When Fox was taken ill, Stone took over the band, and from 1932 it became his, remaining at the Monseigneur Restaurant till 1933. Among its star musicians were Nat Gonella (tpt/voc), Joe Crossman (alto/clt), Tiny Winters (bs/voc), Lew Davis (tmb), Bill Harty (drs), and Al Bowlly (voc). An engagement at the Café Anglais followed, then a move back to the Monseigneur. At the same

Paul Whiteman

time Lew was writing music for films. 1934 spent touring, 1935 at the Hollywood Restaurant, and 1936 touring. From 1937 he gave up the band and concentrated on work as Musical Director for numerous London shows, though continuing to broadcast with session musicians. Gradually however, the size of the band began to decrease, and 1940–42 saw him with a seven-piece at the Dorchester Hotel. Tours and residencies, some with a large band again, followed from 1942–55, and although he kept active until his death in 1969, none of his later bands ever approached the great days of 1931–38. For further details on his style of music *see* our historical section, p. 53–4.

Webb, William 'Chick' (drs, 1909–1939) Born Baltimore, Maryland. Started to play drums and joined local boys' band at age 11. First professional job on pleasure steamers. Moved to New York *c* 1925, and after playing with a few bands began leading his own small groups in clubs. Between 1927 and 1931 gradually increased size of band for various dates and started famous residency at Harlem's Savoy Ballroom 1931. With breaks for other work (in 1932 they accompanied Louis Armstrong on a tour) Chick's band was basically the Savoy's 'House band' until 1938. It was in 1935 that he discovered and introduced Ella Fitzgerald, who briefly took over the band after his death in 1939. He was a hunchback, being barely able to reach his bass drum pedal, and it was tuberculosis of the spine that killed him. Records left behind by the Webb band show that it was a fine, swinging outfit, and Webb one of the great Big Band drummers of all time, not because he was a great technician, but because he laid down such a solid beat. His best epitaph perhaps comes from Gene Krupa. Writing of the occasion in 1937 when the Benny Goodman band had been booked to play a 'battle of the bands' against Chick's at the Savoy he said: '. . . he just cut me to ribbons—made me feel awfully small. When he felt like it he could cut down any of us.'

Whiteman, Paul (vln, 1890–1967) Born Denver, Colorado. Details of his early life and the formation of his Orchestra will be found in our historical section, pages 16–20. By the time the Big Band era was under way, Whiteman had already been a bandleader for many years. It is because of the enormous influence his music had on those who followed him that he finds a place in this book, and that is why so much space in our history is devoted to him. It is regretted that space prevents us from elaborating further on this remarkable man.

THE PLACES, THE PHRASES

Big Bands   This is almost as difficult to define as Swing. Within the terms of reference for this book it generally means bands of not less than 3 trumpets, 2 trombones, 4 saxes and 3 or 4 rhythm, and not more than 4 trumpets, 4 trombones, 5 saxes and 4 rhythm. There are odd exceptions at either end of the scale. In terms commonly accepted by the public in the 1970s, the Big Bands really mean the Swing bands, i.e. post Benny Goodman.

Café Anglais   London restaurant of the 1930s noted as a venue for good dance music, e.g. Roy Fox, Lew Stone, Harry Roy.

Carnegie Hall   New York's premier concert hall. Probably first used for popular music when James Europe (*see* under Bandleaders) presented a concert there in March 1914. However the classic connotation in connection with the Big Bands is undoubtedly Benny Goodman's concert there on 16th January 1938 (*see* Discography).

Cotton Club   One of New York's premier venues for Big Bands, and where Duke Ellington made his name; it was situated on Lenox Avenue in Harlem, New York's black quarter. Some of the most spectacular revues of all time were presented there. Although the shows were invariably all black, the clientèle was usually white. In the 1920s it was the 'in' thing to go to Harlem for your entertainment, a fact which often caused resentment among blacks, since Harlem was basically desperately poor. One recalls the line of Lorenz Hart's lyric for Richard Rodgers' *The Lady is a Tramp*, 'Don't go to Harlem in ermine and pearls. . . .' The Cotton Club itself was even run by a white syndicate, certainly in its prohibition days. Not to be confused with a later establishment, the Cotton Club downtown, which was on Broadway.

Double, Doubling To play more than one musical instrument, e.g., tenor sax and clarinet, or alto doubling baritone. Can also be used of a band doubling 2 venues, e.g., playing a theatre from say, 8–11 pm, and a club or ballroom from midnight to 2 am.

Downbeat American music business magazine, specializing in news, information and reviews about Jazz, bands, and their musicians.

The Cotton Club, Harlem

Inside the Cotton Club: a dance routine by Whyte's Hopping Maniacs

Embassy Club In London's Bond Street. Another important venue for British bands, and where Ambrose made his name in the 1920s. Much patronized at the time by the then Prince of Wales.

Glen Island Casino Another of New York's premier band venues, this time dating from the 1930s. It was here that Glenn Miller really 'made it'. Every band of note wanted to play Glen Island, if only because an engagement there automatically carried with it something like 8–10 broadcasts per week. Situated in New Rochelle.

Harlem New York's black quarter, situated on the East side, very roughly bounded by St. Nicholas' Avenue, 110th St., and the Harlem River.

Jazz Within the context of this book, used in the sense of Jazz choruses, i.e., a musician improvising a chorus on his own within the framework provided by the arranger. A Jazz orientated band is one that appears to have its roots firmly planted in the area of improvisation. Duke Ellington's band was usually referred to in this way.

Killer-Diller Slang term to describe a really swinging arrangement, usually one featuring a lot of high brass and with a loud finale! Its origin is obscure, but it is thought it may have been invented by music critics in the American trade press to describe some of Jimmy Mundy's scores for the Benny Goodman band.

Mayfair Hotel Situated in London's Berkeley Street, and an important venue for British bands in the 1930s. The scene of triumphs for Ambrose, Harry Roy and Jack Jackson.

Meadowbrook Sometimes called Frank Dailey's Meadowbrook. He was the owner. A venue of great importance to the American bands of the Swing Era, since like Glen Island Casino it carried with it an automatic 8–10 broadcasts per week. Ballroom, situated in New Jersey.

Metronome American music business magazine, similar in importance to *Downbeat* (*see* above). Both magazines used to run annual polls of readers' favourite bands and musicians. *Metronome* slightly more Big Band orientated than *Downbeat*, which catered a lot for Jazz. *Metronome* poll winners often ended on an All-Stars recording session.

Monseigneur Restaurant Situated in London's Jermyn Street. Of importance in the history of British bands because it was opened in 1931 by Roy Fox, and was the venue where Lew Stone made his name.

Palomar Ballroom In Los Angeles; commonly accepted as the birth place of Swing during Benny Goodman's stay there in 1935.

Plunger Mute A rubber cup used by trumpet players (and trombone players), which can be moved close or far off the bell of the instrument, thus creating different tones and textures. So called because it looks like the plunger used for unstopping drains! Also referred to as a Wah-wah mute, because of the sound created with it.

Roseland Ballroom A dance hall famous for its employment of the Big Bands, both white and black, and where, among others, Fletcher Henderson made his name. Situated on Broadway.

Inside the Savoy Ballroom: Cootie Williams and his band

Savoy Ballroom One of New York's most famous venues for black bands, situated in Harlem, on Lenox Avenue. Where Chick Webb and Ella Fitzgerald made their names.

Savoy Hotel Situated in London's Strand. Played a leading part in the booking of bands and the playing of dance music since the immediate post-First World War days. In spite of its society clientèle its bookings were sometimes quite adventurous, especially Fred Elizalde.

Swing Many attempts have been made to define it, and frequently they are contradictory. Within the terms of reference of this book it could be said to describe the Swing Era of the Big Bands which started with Benny Goodman at the Palomar Ballroom in Los Angeles, in 1935. But the best definition was given by Fats Waller. When asked what it was he replied: 'Lady, if you gotta ask, you ain't got it!'

173

THE SINGERS

SINGER	BAND(S)
Anderson, Ivie	Duke Ellington
Bailey, Mildred	Paul Whiteman, Red Norvo
Bowlly, Al	Roy Fox, Lew Stone, Ray Noble
Becke, Eve	Jack Hylton
Browne, Sam	Ambrose
Carless, Dorothy	Geraldo
Carlisle, Elsie	Ambrose
Carpenter, Paul	Ted Heath
Carr, Carole	Geraldo
Christy, June	Stan Kenton
Clooney, Rosemary	Tony Pastor
Como, Perry	Ted Weems
Costa, Sam	Maurice Winnick
Crosby, Bing	Paul Whiteman
Dall, Evelyn	Ambrose
Day, Doris	Les Brown
Dell, Peggy	Jack Hylton
Dennis, Denny	Roy Fox, Tommy Dorsey
Eberle, Ray	Glenn Miller
Eberly, Bob	Jimmy Dorsey
Eckstine, Billy	Earl Hines
Fitzgerald, Ella	Chick Webb
Forrest, Helen	Benny Goodman, Artie Shaw, Harry James
Gibbs, Georgia (Fredda Gibson)	Artie Shaw
Gorme, Eydie	Tex Beneke
Hall, Adelaide	Duke Ellington
Haymes, Dick	Harry James, Tommy Dorsey, Benny Goodman
Hibbler, Al	Duke Ellington

Holiday, Billie	Count Basie
Horne, Lena	Noble Sissle, Charlie Barnet
Humes, Helen	Count Basie
Hunter, Alberta	Jack Jackson
Hutton, Marion	Glenn Miller
Kallen, Kitty	Artie Shaw, Jimmy Dorsey
Laine, Cleo	Johnny Dankworth
Lee, Peggy	Benny Goodman
Lenner, Anne	Carroll Gibbons
Leonard, Jack	Tommy Dorsey
Lotis, Dennis	Ted Heath
Lynn, Vera	Ambrose
O'Connell, Helen	Jimmy Dorsey
O'Day, Anita	Gene Krupa, Stan Kenton
O'Malley, Pat	Jack Hylton
Roza, Lita	Ted Heath
Rushing, Jimmy	Count Basie
Shelton, Anne	Ambrose
Sinatra, Frank	Harry James, Tommy Dorsey
Stafford, Jo	Tommy Dorsey
Starr, Kay	Charlie Barnet
Tilton, Martha	Benny Goodman
Torme, Mel	Artie Shaw
Trent, Bruce	Jack Hylton
Valentine, Dickie	Ted Heath
Vaughan, Sarah	Earl Hines
Ward, Helen	Benny Goodman, Harry James, Gene Krupa, Bob Crosby
Warren, Fran	Charlie Barnet, Claude Thornhill
Washington, Dinah	Lionel Hampton
Wayne, Frances	Woody Herman
Williams, Joe	Count Basie, Lionel Hampton
Wright, Edythe	Tommy Dorsey

Jimmy Dorsey and his Orchestra in the film *Hollywood Canteen*, 1944

AN ABBREVIATED DISCOGRAPHY

The records selected are the personal choice of the author. Within the confines of so small a book they cannot begin to be comprehensive. Also, record companies are notoriously quixotic in their selection of records for retention or deletion in their catalogues. At the time of going to press, every effort was made to check the availability of the records listed. Those thought to be deleted are marked with an asterisk*.

It is regretted that so many of them have had to be marked as deleted, but in the interest of historical accuracy it was felt that these should be listed. Second-hand copies may sometimes be available. Also, deleted items do get reissued from time to time, or, as copyrights get reassigned, may reappear on other labels. Nowadays most large cities have specialist record shops who will try to obtain deleted records or foreign imports. To assist collectors the following abbreviations have been used for all records not originated in the UK: **F**, France; **G**, West Germany; **D**, Denmark; **US**, USA.

BRITISH AND AMERICAN BIG BANDS

Ambrose
London Jazz Scene: The 30s (with Lew Stone), Ace of Clubs ACL 1103*
The Bands that Matter, Eclipse ECM 2044
1928–1932, World Records SHB21
Saturday Night, Decca DDV 5003/4

Barnet, Charlie
Charlie Barnet, Vols 1–2, RCA RD 7965*/8088*
Charlie Barnet, Vol. 1, First Heard FHR 12
Skyliner, Pye GH 868

Basie, Count
Rock-a-Bye Basie, Vogue VJD 503
The Best of Basie, Roulette 2682 047
Superchief, CBS M 67205
Jumpin' at the Woodside, Ace of Hearts AH 111*
Atomic Mr Chairman, Vogue VJD 517
Montreux '77, Pablo 2303 207

Brown, Les
The Les Brown Story (1959 remakes), Capitol T 1174*
Concert at the Palladium, Coral LVA 9001/2*
Masters of Swing, Vol. 5 (recorded 1956–59), EMI CO54
81 712 (G)
One-night Stand, Joyce LP 1020

Casa Loma Orchestra
Smoke Rings, Decca DL 8570* (US)
Glen Gray and the Original Casa Loma's Greatest Hits, Decca
DL 75016* (US)
Casa Loma Orchestra 1935-7, Fanfare 11-111

Coon-Sanders Nighthawks
Radio's Aces, RCA LSA 3068*

Cotton, Billy
Billy Cotton and His Band, World Records SH 141

Crosby, Bob
Bob Crosby and His Orchestra (1936–56), Coral LVA 9045*
The Radio Years, London HMG 5021
South Rampart St. Parade, MCA MCFM 2578

Dorsey Brothers Orchestra
Bring Back the Good Times, MCA/Coral 6 28315 DP (G)
Fabulous Dorseys Play Dixieland Jazz, Coral CP 27*
The Fabulous Dorseys in Hi-Fi, Philips BBL 7295*

Dorsey, Jimmy
The Fabulous JD, HMV CLP 1132*
The Radio Years, London HMG 5022
Remember Jimmy, Decca DL 74248* (US)
Jimmy Dorsey Orchestra 1944-7, First Heard 4

Dorsey, Tommy
TD and his Orchestra, Vols 1–2, RCA DPM 2026/2042
The Best of TD, Vols 1–2, RCA 731 129/741 053 (F)
Tommy Dorsey 1938–41, RCA Black and White FXM
42036 (F)

With Vocals by Frank Sinatra, RCA HY 1015

Elizalde, Fred
Jazz at the Savoy, Ace of Clubs ACL 1102*

Ellington, Duke
Cotton Club Days, Vols 1–2, Ace of Hearts AH 23*/AH 89*
The Duke 1889–1974, CBS 88077
The Age of Ellington, RCA PL 42086
Toodle-oo, Vocalion VLP 4
70th Birthday Concert, United Artists UAD 60001/2
Golden Duke, RCA PR 24029*
The World of Duke Ellington, CBS 88128

Fox, Roy
Fox Favourites, Ace of Clubs ACL 1240
At the Monseigneur, Ace of Clubs ACL 1172
The Bands that Matter, Eclipse ECM 2045
Roy Fox 1936–38, World Records SH 331/2

Geraldo
Geraldo and his Orchestra, World Records SH 215

Gibbons, Carroll
The Carroll Gibbons Story, World Records SH 167/8

Goldkette, Jean
Dance Hits of the 20s (re-creations by Sy Oliver), RCA/
Camden CDN 154*

Goodman, Benny
The Best of BG, RCA SF 8001*
All Time Greatest Hits, CBS 67268
Charlie Christian with BG, CBS 52538*
Benny Rides Again, Columbia 33SX 1038*
Benny Goodman Today, Decca DDS 3
The Kingdom of Swing, RCA LPM 2247* (US)
The Best of Benny Goodman, RCA HY 1020
1938 Carnegie Hall Jazz Concert, CBS 66202

Greatest Swing Band in the World
The Greatest Swing Band in the World, Pye NSPL 18492
Yes Indeed, Pye NSPL 18493

Hampton, Lionel
Hamp's Golden Favourites, Decca DL 74296* (US)
The Big Band Sound of Lionel Hampton, Verve 2317 079*
Hamp's Big Band, Audio Fidelity 5913 (US)

Lionel, Audio Fidelity 5849 (US)
Lionel Hampton, Vol 6, MCA 510 140

Heath, Ted
The Big Band World of Ted Heath, Decca SPA 54
100th London Palladium Concert, Eclipse ECS 2091
At the London Palladium, Eclipse ECS 2164

Henderson, Fletcher
A Study in Frustration, Vols 1–4, CBS 62001–4*
Fletcher Henderson 1927–36, RCA 730 584 (F)

Herman, Woody
The Band that Plays the Blues, Ace of Hearts AH 156*
The Thundering Herd, Vols 1–3, CBS 62158–60*
Greatest Hits, CBS 52551
40th Anniversary Concert, Carnegie Hall 1976, RCA PL 02203
Woody Herman (recorded 1948–50), Capitol M 11034 (US)

Hylton, Jack
Jack Hylton, Ace of Clubs ACL 1205
The Band that Jack Built, World Records SH 190
The Bands that Matter, Eclipse ECM 2046
Jack's Back, Encore ENC 162*

Jackson, Jack
Make Those People Sway, World Records SH 210

James, Harry
The Hits of Harry James, Starline SRS 5049
Beat of the Big Bands, Embassy EMB 31048
Harry James and his Orchestra, Fanfare 9–109
The Young Harry James, Jazz Archives JA 31

Jones, Isham
The Great Isham Jones Orchestra, RCA RD 7643*
Swingin' Down the Lane, Ace of Hearts AH 110*
Isham Jones and his Orchestra, Sunbeam HB 306

Kaempfert, Bert
Love Walked In, Polydor 2310 430
Everybody Loves Somebody, Polydor 2482 288
Contemporary Kaempfert, Polydor 2310 456

Kenton, Stan
Stan Kenton's Greatest Hits, Capitol CAP 1002
Stan Kenton in Hi-Fi, Capitol LCT 6109*

Today—Live in London, Decca DML 3 1/2

Krupa, Gene
Drummin' Man, CBS 62289–90*
The Radio Discs of Gene Krupa, Joyce LP 2008 (US)
The Best of Gene Krupa, Verve 68594 (US)
Gene Krupa 1938–42, Fanfare 10–110

Last, James
10 Years Non-Stop, Polydor 2660 111
Non-Stop Dancing 17, Polydor 2371 626

Lawrence, Syd
Swing's Greatest Hits 1976, Philips 9109 209
The Music of Glenn Miller, Philips 6641 017
Spotlight on Syd Lawrence, Philips 6625 029 CB

Lombardo, Guy
Guy Lombardo in Hi-Fi, Capitol LCT 6117*
The Sweetest Music this Side of Heaven, Ace of Hearts
AH 86*
New Year's Eve with Guy Lombardo, Decca PFS 4238

Lunceford, Jimmie
Rhythm is Our Business, Ace of Hearts AH 155*
Harlem Shout, Decca DL 79238* (US)
For Dancers Only, Decca DL 79239* (US)
Blues in the Night, Decca DL 79240* (US)
The Golden Years, Storyville SLP 828

McKinney's Cotton Pickers
McKinney's Cotton Pickers, RCA RD 7561*

Miller, Glenn
Unforgettable, RCA TVL 1
The Army Air Force Band, RCA DHY 0004
A Memorial 1944–69, RCA GM 1
The Glenn Miller Story, RCA LSA 3274
The Legendary Glenn Miller
   Vols 1–4, RCA LFM 1 7500–3
   Vols 5–9, RCA LFM 1 7512–6
   Vols 10–13, RCA LSA 3237–40

Million Airs
The Million Airs, Buk BULP 2006
Five Flats Unfurnished, Buk BULP 2013

New Big Band
Today in the Old Fashioned Way, Decca PFS 4417

New Paul Whiteman Orchestra
Runnin' Wild, Argo ZDA 167
Music of the Roaring 20s, Wave LP 27

Noble, Ray
Ray Noble and his Orchestra, RCA RD 7881*
Ray Noble Plays Ray Noble, World Records SH 198

Rich, Buddy
Plays and Plays and Plays, RCA PL 12273
Buddy Rich and his Greatest Band, First Heard 5*

Roy, Harry
The World of Harry Roy, Decca SPA 141

Savoy Orpheans, Savoy Havana Band
The Savoy Bands, World Records SH 165/6

Shaw, Artie
Concerto for Clarinet, RCA DPM 2028
Artie Shaw and his Musicians 1949, First Heard 6*

Squadronaires
There's Something in the Air, Eclipse ECM 2112
Contrasts in Jazz, Decca LF 1141*

Stone, Lew
10.30 Tuesday Night, Ace of Clubs ACL 1147
London Jazz Scene: the 30s (with Ambrose), Ace of Clubs
ACL 1103*
The Bands that Matter, Eclipse ECM 2047
Lew Stone and his Band, Decca DDV 5005/6

Thornhill, Claude
Snowfall, Monmouth Evergreen MRS 6006 (US)

Webb, Chick
Spinning the Webb, Coral CP 3*
The Legend, Decca DL 79222* (US)
King of the Savoy, Decca DL 79223* (US)

Whiteman, Paul
Paul Whiteman's 50th Anniversary Record, Music For
Pleasure MFP 1183*
Paul Whiteman, Vols 1–2, RCA RD 7954*/8090*
Paul Whiteman and his Orchestra, RCA DPM 2077*

EUROPEAN BIG BANDS

Edelhagen, Kurt (West Germany)
Toast to the Bands, Contour 2870 114
Big Band Swing, Carnival 2941 305*

Francis Bey Orchestra (Belgium)
Hits of Basie and Ellington, Saga EROS 8012*

The Francy Boland Orchestra (France)
MPC DC 229 106 (F)

Ramblers (Netherlands)
With Coleman Hawkins, Ace of Clubs ACL 1247*

Ventura, Ray (France)
Music Made in France, Saga STM 6014*
Paris I Love You, Society SOC 934*

Anthologies
Danske Guldalder Jazz (Denmark), Vols 1–4, Odeon
MOCK 1006–9* (D)
Jazz in Deutschland (West Germany), Vols 1–6, Historia
H630 5* (G)
La Pré-histoire du Jazz en France (France), Pathé CO54
10656* (F)
Swing from Belgium (Belgium), Swingfan 1002* (G)

ANTHOLOGIES

This is the Big Bands, RCA DPS 2019 (2 LP set)
Big Bands Greatest Hits, Vol. 1, CBS 66268 (2 LP set)
Big Bands Greatest Hits, Vol. 2, CBS 67292 (2 LP set)
16 Big Band Greats, Vols 1–2, MCA/Coral CDLM 8024/
8046*
Dazzling Jazz—the Big Sound, Philips BBL 7209*
Dance Bands on the Air, Vols 1–2, BBC REC 139M/140M
The Golden Age of British Dance Bands:
    1925–7, World Records SH 361
    1927–31, World Records SH 362
    1931–4, World Records SH 363
    1934–6, World Records SH 364
    1936–8, World Records SH 365
    1938–9, World Records SH 366

The Golden Age of British Dance Bands (Roy Fox, Harry Roy, Lew Stone, Ray Noble), World Records SH 118/9
Kings of Swing: 1937–46, Verve 2352 074/6*
Kings of Swing: 1946–60, Verve 2367 210/11*
The World of Swing, Vols 1–2, CBS 88134
1926, 1927, 1928 (3 Vols), RCA LSA 3075/77/78*
Paper Moon (soundtrack), Paramount SPFL 290
Makin' Whoopee, World Records SH 229
And the Bands Played On, Decca DDV 5001/2
Swing, RCA DHY 001
The Roaring 20s, Vine VMP 1022
The Swing Era (re-creations by Billy May and Glen Gray), Vols 1–15, 1930s to 1970s, Time-Life STL 340–354 (available on subscription only)

BIBLIOGRAPHY

Barnes, Ken, *Sinatra and the Great Song Stylists* (1972); Ian Allen Ltd.
Chilton, John, *Who's Who of Jazz* (1970); Bloomsbury Bookshop, London
Colin, Sid, *And the Bands Played On* (1977); Elm Tree Books
Connor and Hicks, *Benny Goodman on the Record* (1969); Arlington House, New York
Crosby, Bing, *Call Me Lucky* (1955); Frederick Muller Ltd.
Dance, Stanley, *The World of Duke Ellington* (1971); Macmillan & Co.
Flower, John, *Moonlight Serenade* (1972); Arlington House, New York
Goodman and Kolodin, *The Kingdom of Swing* (1961); Frederick Ungar Publishing Co., New York
Jackson, Arthur, *The World of Big Bands* (1977); David & Charles Ltd.
Jewell, Derek, *Duke* (1971); Elm Tree Books
Jones and Chilton, *Louis* (1971); November Books Ltd.

Jørgensen and Wiedemann, *Jazzens Hvem-Hvad-Hvor* (1962); Politikens Forlag, Copenhagen

Lang, Horst, *Die Geschichte des Jazz in Deutschland* (1960); Verlag Uhle & Kleimann, Lübbecke

Lang, Horst, *Jazz in Deutschland 1900–1960* (1966); Colloquium Verlag, Berlin

McCarthy, Albert, *The Dance Band Era* (1971); Studio Vista

McCarthy, Albert, *Big Band Jazz* (1974); Studio Vista

McCarthy, Harrison, Morgan and Oliver, *Jazz on Record 1917–1967* (1968); Hanover Books

Nelson, Stanley, *All About Jazz* (1934); Heath Cranton

Rust, Brian, *The Dance Bands* (1972); Ian Allen Ltd.

Sanford, Herb, *Tommy and Jimmy—The Dorsey Years* (1972); Ian Allen Ltd.

Schwaninger and Gurwitsch, *Swing Discographie* (1946); Ch. Grasset, Geneva

Shaw, Artie, *The Trouble with Cinderella*, (1952); Farrar, Strauss & Young, New York

Simon, George T., *Glenn Miller and His Orchestra* (1974); W. H. Allen & Co.

Simon, George T., *The Big Bands* (1974); Collier Books, New York

INDEX

Page numbers in **bold** type refer to illustrations.

188

189